VENUS OBSERVED

CHRISTOPHER FRY

VENUS OBSERVED

A Play

OXFORD UNIVERSITY PRESS

NEW YORK AND LONDON

FIFTH PRINTING, 1952

Printed in the United States of America

TO PHYL
my wife

CHARACTERS

(in order of their appearance)

THE DUKE OF ALTAIR

EDGAR, *his son*

HERBERT REEDBECK, *his agent*

DOMINIC, *Reedbeck's son*

ROSABEL FLEMING

JESSIE DILL

CAPTAIN FOX REDDLEMAN,
  the Duke's butler

BATES, *the Duke's footman*

HILDA TAYLOR-SNELL

PERPETUA, *Reedbeck's daughter*

SCENES

The Observatory Room at Stellmere
Park, the Duke's mansion

The Temple of the Ancient Virtues,
Stellmere Park

ACT ONE

*A room at the top of a mansion: once a bedroom, now an observatory.
When the curtain rises the* DUKE OF ALTAIR *is in argument
with his son* EDGAR. *Also present is* HERBERT REEDBECK, *the*
DUKE'S *agent.*

DUKE. Anyone would think I had made some extraordinary
Suggestion. But in fact how natural it is.
Aren't you my son?

EDGAR.   Yes, father, of course I am.

DUKE. Then it's up to you to choose who shall be your mother.
Does that seem to you improper, Reedbeck?

REEDBECK.   No,
Your Grace; it's not, perhaps, always done,
But few parents consider their children as you do.
I don't dislike the plan at all.

EDGAR.   I sweat
With embarrassment.

DUKE.   You have been
Too much with the horses. This, that I ask you to do,
Is an act of poetry, and a compliment
To the freshness of your mind. Why should you sweat?
Here they will be, three handsome women,
All of them at some time implicated
In the joyous routine of my life. (I could scarcely
Put it more delicately.) I wish to marry.
Who am I, in heaven's name, to decide
Which were my vintage years of love?

[1]

Good God, to differentiate between
The first bright blow on my sleeping flesh,
The big breasts of mid-morning,
And the high old dance of afternoon—
Value one against the other? Never, not I,
Till the eschatological rain shall lay my dust.
But you, dear boy, with your twenty-five impartial years,
Can perform the judgement of Paris,
Can savour, consider, and award the apple
With a cool hand. You will find an apple
Over there by the spectroscope.

EDGAR.   But why must you marry?
Or, if that's an impertinence, why do I have to have
A mother? I've been able to grow to a sizable boy
Without one.

DUKE.   Why? Because I see no end
To the parcelling out of heaven in small beauties,
Year after year, flocks of girls, who look
So lately kissed by God
They come out on the world with lips shining,
Flocks and generations, until time
Seems like nothing so much
As a blinding snowstorm of virginity,
And a man, lost in the perpetual scurry of white,
Can only close his eyes
In a resignation of monogamy.

EDGAR. Anyway, it would be an impossibly hasty
Judgement. Honour you as I may, I don't
See how I can do it.

DUKE.   If Paris had no trouble
Choosing between the tide-turning beauty,
Imponderable and sexed with eternity,

Of Aphrodite, Hera, and Athene,
Aren't you ashamed to make heavy weather of a choice
Between Hilda, and Rosabel, and Jessie?
And if you can't make up your mind about a woman
At first meeting, all hope of definition has gone;
Prejudice, delirium, or rage
Will cock their snooks, and the apple will go bad.
No, boy, no; go and water your horses
And come back and choose your mother.

EDGAR.   At what time?

DUKE. What is it now?

REEDBECK.   Five past eleven.

DUKE.   They should
Be here. At eleven twenty-nine we're to have
The total eclipse of the sun, to which I've invited them.
The mouth of the moon has already begun to munch.
We shall all feel ourselves making a north-west passage
Through the sea of heaven, and darkness will cover
The face of the earth. In that moment
All women will be as one.

EDGAR.   That's what I was going
To ask you. I don't want to play the heavy son,
But would you say you loved these women equally?

DUKE. Equality is a mortuary word. Just choose.
Shall I be happy on Tuesdays, Thursdays, and Saturdays,
Or on Mondays, Wednesdays, and Fridays? Some such difference
Is all that your choice involves.

Enter CAPTAIN FOX REDDLEMAN, *a manservant. He looks like,
and was once, a lion tamer.*

REDDLEMAN.   'Scuse, your Grace:
But a telegram for our little friend Mr. Reedbeck.

[3]

A telegram, Mr. Reedbeck. B'Jason, four
Flights I've had to come up to bring it to you.
Please Jenny it's worth it. And the boy's waiting.

EDGAR. Well, father, I don't know; with a certain sense
Of preconceiving myself, I may come back.
I shall do what I can for you; I only hope
You'll not live to regret the way my fancy
Takes you.

[*Exit* EDGAR.

REEDBECK. Oh! Would you ever think
Such a joy could happen to me, in the world as we know it?

REDDLEMAN. I have to tell your Grace, in all decency
To the footman Bates, who I religiously despise,
If the fellow comes on duty with a bloody nose
'Tis my doing, and long may it bleed. And h'wot
About the boy below, Mr. Reedbeck? Any answer?

REEDBECK. No, no, Reddleman, only thanksgiving.
Oh, and I suppose a shilling, he'd like a shilling.

DUKE. And go gently with Bates, Reddleman, or else
You'll drive him back to his old nervous habits
Of biting his nails and burglary. Remember
You're not a lion tamer now.

REDDLEMAN.   And that
Was a hit below—I'm wearing no belt—below
The navel. Thank God I'm severed from my mother
Or she would have felt it severely. I'd remind you
'Twas fighting for king and country I lost me nerve,
And b'Daniel, it's a sad job to be parted
From the lords of the jungle.

DUKE.   I'm sorry, Reddleman;
I wasn't meaning to hurt you.

[4]

REDDLEMAN.   Well, go easy,
Go easy with me, your Grace. Now, Mr. Reedbeck:
Thanksgiving and a bob for the boy below:
Very good.

[*Exit* REDDLEMAN.

REEDBECK.   A red-letter day for me, your Grace;
Let me see: the twenty-ninth of October?

DUKE.   Yes;
The leaves transfigured by the thought of death,
The wind south-west, a blue sky buffaloed
By cloud, the sun approaching its eclipse.

REEDBECK. You remember I have a daughter? I've spoken of her
From time to time; I had the astounding fortune
To beget her, as though I'd been chosen to release
A rose from the world's rock; and then I had
The misery to lose her, when her mother
Left me for America, ten years ago.
Well, now I'm holding in my hand a message
Which says she's returning to me, returning to-day,
No time of arrival, just bare and astonishing
'Am in England hope to kiss you before lunch
Perpetua.' I can hardly believe it could happen,
I can't believe so, not in the world as we know it.

DUKE. Go easy, Reedbeck, go easy with yourself.

REEDBECK. If she should come in time for the eclipse——

DUKE. Then, of course, she shall join us to see the eclipse.
It will be a change for her after America.
I'm going now, to dress. Subdue yourself, Reedbeck.
Otherwise you'll capsize in disappointment.
Expect the worst.

[*Exit the* DUKE.

REEDBECK.   Not at all, oh, no, not at all,
No shadows of that sort.

> *[He hums to the telephone.*

Must warn my housekeeper.
'I galloped, Dirck galloped, we galloped all three . . .'
Oh, Mrs. Lendy, Mr. Reedbeck here; I have to ask you
To prepare a room for my daughter. I'm so glad
To hear you gasp. However, we must keep our heads,
Such as they are. Tell her to join us here
And ask to be shown to the Observatory Room.
There will be refreshment for her, and a total
Eclipse of the sun.

Enter DOMINIC, REEDBECK's *son.*

DOMINIC.   I want to speak to you.
How long are we likely to be alone?

REEDBECK.   In a moment,
Dominic dear. You'll put her some flowers, Mrs. Lendy.
Are the Helianthus gone? Well, *uliginosum.*
You call them chrysanthemums, I think. And on her bed
The lilac linen sheets. Some time before lunch.
Good-bye. Oh, Dominic, my dear, dear boy,
Your sister's coming home!

DOMINIC *[silent, and then].*   That makes you happy.

REEDBECK. Oh, dear, it's one of your knock-the-bottom-
Out-of-everything mornings. Or do you mean
You've heard, and you know what's bringing her home?
I hope nothing's amiss?

DOMINIC.   Not with her.

REEDBECK.   Well, then——

DOMINIC. Do I say what I have to say *here*? Or do we go back
To the house? It isn't going to be pleasant.

[6]

REEDBECK.   Of course it is.
There's nothing unpleasant that isn't going to be pleasant.
Perpetua's returning to me; the world
Is no longer depressed at the poles, and everything
Will be pleasant: the east wind, smoking fires,
Revolution, debility——

DOMINIC.   Jail?

REEDBECK.   Yes, jail,
Solitary confinement, the cat-o'-nine-tails,
Your Aunt Florence——

DOMINIC.   Can you keep your feet
On sober earth for five difficult minutes
And talk responsibly? Why are we so rich?
I've asked you before; but you, a Duke's bailiff,
An agent: where did our money come from?

REEDBECK. Have you no capacity for delight?
Do for all our sakes be pleasant, dear boy.

DOMINIC. You said our money came from legacies, you told me
From legacies!

REEDBECK.   Just so, we've been very fortunate.
Your Uncle Hector, when he put on immortality
In Tasmania, increased, to a certain extent,
Our freedom from care; and old Lady Bright, my first
Employer, when she passed on, passed on
Herself to heaven and the rest to me; and then——

DOMINIC. I have to ask for figures. My Uncle Hector
Died, leaving——?

REEDBECK.   Don't let's talk of death.
I've a heart this morning as light as a nebula.
But you, you sombre boy, you can't even

[7]

Sputter up a few sparks when I tell you
Your sister's coming home!

DOMINIC. Died, leaving——?

REEDBECK. Really,
How can I be expected to remember?
There was some music, certainly; the piano score
Of *The Quaker Girl*; and I recollect some ninepins;
And a small South American lizard called Faithful
Which died in quarantine. But Lady Bright——

DOMINIC. You've stolen the money, haven't you: steadily
And consistently? O God, why ask? I know
Already. And thieved with so little subtlety
Anyone might know. Raised rents
But entered in your books at the old figure;
Sale of produce and timber, at prices higher
Than you've recorded. I've been ferreting,
Ever since an unmistakable innuendo
From Bates the footman.

REEDBECK. Come now; Bates
Is a common burglar, and sees, of course,
His reflection in all about him. He was caught
Red-handed with the silver, and his Grace,
Being short of staff at the time, asked him to stay
And clean it.

DOMINIC. Bates is quite a decent fellow.
I've had a long talk to him. He used to suffer
From a pathological lust for climbing ladders
And had to rationalize it when he got
To the top. And now he's determined to be honest,
Even if it makes him ill, he says. But with you
It's unrelieved, wicked cupidity.
Of course I go down from Cambridge. I couldn't stay there

[8]

When any morning I might wake up and find
I'd become the son of a convict. We're both in
For misery now, and Perpetua comes home
Just in time to share it.

REEDBECK.   I wish I could explain
How very mistaken I'm sure you must be. Especially
On such a cheerful morning. It's really too bad.
We have the dark every twelve hours as it is
Without inventing more.

Enter BATES: *he shows a trace of rough handling. He announces* MISS
ROSABEL FLEMING, *and withdraws.*

ROSABEL. I expected to find the Duke here.

REEDBECK.   The competitors!
I'd forgotten them. You'll forgive me, madam, I hope;
You find me a little disjunct. His Grace
Will join us shortly. My name is Reedbeck.
This was my son.

ROSABEL.   Was your son?

REEDBECK.   There's no
Other tense for me now except the past,
Miss Belmont. You were Miss Belmont?

ROSABEL.   Rosabel Fleming.
I am still Rosabel Fleming.

DOMINIC.   Please excuse me.
I'd like to know you, but I can't look anyone
Happily in the eye. I'm pleased to have met you.

[*Exit* DOMINIC.

ROSABEL. Is he in trouble?

REEDBECK.   The paradoxes of virtue
Have confused him. Won't you sit down, Miss Fleming?

[9]

ROSABEL. I begin to understand why the theatre
Gives me so little work.
That could scarcely have been called a splendid entrance,
Even by the most loving.

REEDBECK.   Go down from Cambridge.
Did you hear him say that? No, you were not here.
It let all the life out of me for a moment.
All the Latin I have myself, you know,
Is horticultural: *muscari comosum*
Monstrosum, and *scrophularia nodosa*,
Et cetera ad infinitum. But how I longed
As a boy for the groves and grooves of Academe.
Give me civilization, Miss Fleming; you can keep
Your progress.

ROSABEL.   This room, surely, is something new?

REEDBECK. The Observatory Room, giving upon
An uninterrupted sweep of the Surrey heavens;
At night the weeping stars; by day——

Enter MRS. JESSIE DILL.

JESSIE.   I'm sorry.
I thought it would be just his Grace. I'll go again.

REEDBECK. No, no, his Grace will be here. By day
The brandishing sun inciting the earth
To revolution and rotation——

JESSIE.   I'm Mrs. Dill.
It's my own fault the man hasn't announced me.
It seemed to me 'All those stairs, for the poor young chap
Just to say Here's Jessie.' He went on insisting,
Of course, but when we got to the second landing
He must have thought it was getting a bit undignified
Both of us coming up two steps at a time,

So he slid back down the banisters.
Surely I've met you before, dear?

ROSABEL.   Rosabel Fleming.

JESSIE. I should have remembered. I saw you, once upon a time,
Being very sweet in a play about Ophelia.
And this is a strange thing, too, being up here
In this room together. You'd hardly recognize it.
Well, I don't know, I should say that's a telescope.

ROSABEL. I think I must go. I hadn't understood
The Duke would have visitors. . . .

REEDBECK.   We were just talking
About this room when you came, Mrs. Dill. My name
Is Reedbeck. This was one of his Grace's
Bedrooms, as perhaps. . . . But now, as you see,
He prefers to regard the skies here, scavenging
Through the night for knowledge. He also uses
The room for experiments.

JESSIE.   He always did.

ROSABEL. I've decided not to stay. I only came in
For a moment, finding myself not far away.
If you'd be kind enough to tell him——

Enter the DUKE.

DUKE.   Good morning, Rosabel.
Good morning, Jessie.

JESSIE.   Here he is, himself.
He's the same boy, God bless him, not a day older,
Even if he does have to use a telescope.

DUKE. Flattery, Jessie; for years the frost has lain
On my stubble beard. The swallows and other such
Migratory birds have left me months ago.

[11]

JESSIE. You must build yourself a nice fire.

DUKE.   No, Jessie;
I have to consider my years and decline with the sun,
Gracefully but gratefully decline.
I have also to apologize for keeping you waiting.
I was up all night with the universe again
And slept late. Or is that not to be
Forgiven? A silence broods on Rosabel.

ROSABEL. I was conscious of it. I was wondering
What note to sound. I'm suddenly very uncertain
Why I'm here.

DUKE.   For a total eclipse of the sun.
Didn't I mention it to you in my letter?

ROSABEL. Is there some tradition that old friends should meet
    again
During an eclipse? Or what other reason? Your birthday?
No, you're a Sagittarian. This is only October.

DUKE. And the leaves are falling. What shall a robin do then,
Poor thing?

JESSIE.   Sit in this barn, and keep himself warm,
And tuck himself up alone in the east wing,
Poor thing.

Enter EDGAR.

DUKE.   My son Edgar, Miss Rosabel Fleming.
I introduce Rosabel first, Jessie, to give you
Time to enjoy your joke. My son Edgar,
Mrs. Dill.

JESSIE.   How lovely it is to meet you.
I've known your father, you know, ever since
I was ever so slim. Though, of course, properly speaking,
It was my husband who was really his friend.

[12]

I hope your father will allow me to say
His friend.

DUKE.   I'm delighted to let you say it.
I didn't know he had ever been alive
Or we might have said it before.

EDGAR.   It's just as well
We understand my father.

ROSABEL.   And it's just as well
We don't all have to. It's a thing I have no love for,
To have to go groping along the corridors
Of someone else's mind, so that I shan't
Be hurt. No one has any right to ask it.

DUKE. We're not, I hope, in this mellow October light
Getting ill at ease? We're here this morning to watch
The sun annulled and renewed, and to sit affectionately
Over the year's dilapidation. 'Mellow'
Is the keynote of the hour. We must be mellow,
Remembering we've been on the earth two million years,
Man and boy and Sterkfontein ape.

REEDBECK [singing abstractedly at the window].

            You call me old
            But I am still
      A chippy young chap on Chipperton Hill
            And shall be, while
            My flesh can cover
      The bones of a bona-fide lover.
      Heydilly, heydilly, hang me a sheep.

DUKE. Happy, happy Reedbeck. He has a daughter
Returning to him.

JESSIE.   And there he sits and purrs
As though the morning was a saucer of milk.

[13]

REEDBECK. I caught myself singing. I do beg your pardon.

EDGAR. Sing away, Reedbeck. Bring her in with music.
This is wonderful news.

[BATES *at the door.*

REEDBECK. Can this be—is it . . .?

[BATES *announces, and enter,* MRS. TAYLOR-SNELL.

DUKE. The exact Hilda. Punctuality
Was drawing its last breath. The sun has mooned
Away half its light already.

HILDA.   A party, Hereward?
You didn't tell me.

DUKE.   I scarcely knew. And anyway
We shall all feel quite alone, except, perhaps, Jessie.
Mrs. Dill, Mrs. Taylor-Snell. There will only be
The appearance of people being near to us.
Miss Rosabel Fleming, Mrs. Taylor-Snell.
Reedbeck you know. You've disappointed him.
He hoped you would have been his daughter.

HILDA. Did you ever propose it, Reedbeck?

REEDBECK.   You see before you
A creaking bough on which, at any moment,
A dear young daughter may alight.

DUKE. My extension in time: Edgar.

EDGAR.   Five feet ten
Of my unlimited father.

HILDA.   I have often
Expected to meet you.

EDGAR.   I suppose so;
But until he's dead I'm really a redundancy.
I make him feel bifurcated.

[14]

JESSIE.   Wherever
Does he learn those terrible words?

EDGAR.   I spend
Such a lot of my time in the stables.

DUKE [*to* BATES, *who has loitered by the door*]. What is it, Bates?

BATES.   There are faces
As can be mauled about wiv, and there are faces
As can't be mauled about wiv. Mine can't
Be mauled about wiv. Memo, guvnor, to be 'anded
On to the proper quarters, and *you* know
What basket I refers to.
Will that be all, guvnor?

DUKE.   That will be all, Bates.

> [*Exit* BATES. REEDBECK *throws open the window and leans
> out.*

HILDA. Be careful, Reedbeck! There really is such a thing
As the force of gravity.

REEDBECK.   Only the wind blowing
And the rattle of leaves. I hoped it would prove to be
Internal combustion.

DUKE [*aside to* EDGAR]. I should have mentioned to you,
The case of Athene is minutely complicated
By a husband. But don't be deflected. He would still
Have the shooting over the estate. Nothing
Is insurmountable.

EDGAR.   Except yourself,
I take you to mean. But it's all right;
I'm devoted to you.

HILDA.   Why don't you give it up,
Reedbeck? There's no daughter there. How much
This house has aged, Hereward, since I saw it

[15]

Last. I was thinking so coming up the stairs.
It looks as though the walls have cried themselves
To sleep for nights on end. And the number of windows
Broken! I don't think you should throw nearly
So many stones. The spiders are larger, the jackdaws
Ruder, the servants more eccentric. You mustn't
Drift into Gothic, when your physique is so
Stubbornly Norman.

DUKE.   I see no point in trying
To make time look as though it were standing still
By renewing the face of it. I like to watch my own
Deft and reckless plunge into ancient history.
It assuages my lust for speed. Dark glasses for the ladies,
Reedbeck; tell them to look at the sun.

EDGAR.   And to pray
For all small birds under the eye of the hawk.

JESSIE. I can remember, when I was a kid,
Being got out of bed and told I had to look
At something in the sky. I kept on saying
Oh, yes, mum, isn't it lovely, isn't it lovely?
It was a comet or a zeppelin or something,
But all I could see was the usual end
Of the Crystal Palace.

REEDBECK [*handing glasses*]. Look at the sun, Mrs. Dill.

JESSIE. And now I can't help feeling
As if I'd just been got out of bed again
To look at something I probably shan't see.

DUKE. That's the human predicament, in a nutshell.

ROSABEL. There's a kind of humour abroad this morning that seems to
Put me outside the party.

[16]

REEDBECK.   Look at the sun, Miss Fleming.

ROSABEL. Thank you.

EDGAR.   I've such a feeling of pre-natal
Tension, it's more than a boy can bear. Father,
I'm going to make the decision now
And pin the future down for you.

HILDA.   But will you
Find that easy? I couldn't help overhearing.
The future has the most uncertain temper.
After all you've said, Hereward, do you teach
Your child to tamper with time?

DUKE.   He had it to play with
When he was young; but he'll soon see
How it will rag him to death. Meanwhile, the eclipse.
Let me be your guide. Observe how Sol Salome
Almost hidden by the head of the Baptist moon
Dances her last few steps of fire.

HILDA.   You're confusing
The sex of the sun.

DUKE.   It's the act itself: observe
The copulation of Jove, magnificent in
Mid air.

JESSIE.   The bulk of the moon, creeping on
And on. It makes me feel more solemn than I've ever
Felt before at eleven o'clock in the morning.

EDGAR. No nice eclipse for you, Miss Fleming?

ROSABEL.   Why, yes,
It was what your father invited me to see.
I was far away for the moment.

[17]

EDGAR. Before you go
To the window, I wonder if you'd mind accepting this apple?

ROSABEL. No, thank you. I'll go and see what there is to be seen
Before it's too late.

EDGAR. Father, may I have your attention?
There, Miss Fleming, it will come in useful sometime.

DUKE. Daylight, you see, is shamming twilight. Nature
Is being made a fool of. Three or four stars, there,
You can see them wince, where only a moment earlier
Morning was all serene. The crows, with much
Misgiving, talk themselves into their trees. Even
The usually phlegmatic owls
Care a hoot or two. The bats from the barn
Make one flickering flight, and return to hang
Their heads. All of them tricked and fuddled
By the passing of a small cadaverous planet.

HILDA. Yes, we understand the event perfectly.

JESSIE. Let him enjoy it. Space, ever and ever,
On and on. . . . Well, I don't know.

EDGAR. Father, I don't know whether you have noticed:
A certain event has occurred.

DUKE. Is now occurring.
We're crossing perceptibly into the dark.
Daylight differences are made subordinate
To the general shade.

EDGAR. Father, for God's sake, look!
I am giving Miss Fleming an apple.

ROSABEL. You've already
Given me an apple.

DUKE. I observe you're plying

Rosabel with fruit. *Bis dat qui cito dat.*
We can now turn our attention again to the sun.

EDGAR. So a revolutionary change begins
Without raising a hand's turn of the dust.
Ah, well; give me some dark glass.

HILDA.   What a shame
If that cloud spoils the climax for us.

REEDBECK.   No,
It avoids, you see; it glides mercifully
And dexterously past. I hope and pray
The same will be true of the cloud that hangs over my own
Sunshine: but young men can be so ruthless,
So ruthless; it's terrible to think about.

DUKE. What now, Reedbeck?

REEDBECK.   Ah, yes; to the cosmos it doesn't
Matter; I suppose I agree.

JESSIE.   To think
We're in the shadow of old Lunabella

DUKE.   To think.

JESSIE. When she moves over will she see us
Coming out of her shadow? Are we really
As bright as a moon, from the moon's side of the question?

DUKE. We have a borrowed brilliance. At night
Among the knots and clusters and corner boys
Of the sky, among asteroids and cepheids,
With Sirius, Mercury, and Canis Major,
Among nebulae and magellanic cloud,
You shine, Jessie.

JESSIE.   You're making me self-conscious.

DUKE. Here we're as dull as unwashed plates; out there
We shine. That's a consideration. Come
Close to paradise, and where's the lustre?
But still, at some remove, we shine, and truth
We hope is content to keep a distant prospect.
So you, Jessie, and the swamps of the equator,
Shine; the boring overplus of ocean,
The Walworth Road, the Parthenon, and Reedbeck
Shine; the dark tree with the nightingale
At heart, dockyards, the desert, the newly dead,
Minarets, gasometers, and even I
Fall into space in one not unattractive
Beam. To take us separately is to stare
At mud; only together, at long range,
We coalesce in light.

JESSIE.   I like to think I'm being
A ray of light to some nice young couple out there.
'There's the Great Bear,' they'd say, and 'Look,
There's old Jessie, tilted on her side
Just over the Charing Cross Hotel.'

HILDA.   You both
Chatter so. It's a moment for quiet. Who knows
If ever I'll see this again.

EDGAR.   The end of our lord
The sun.

ROSABEL. It's no good. I must get out into the air!
It's impossible to breathe up here!

DUKE.   What is it,
Rosabel? Claustrophobia on the brink
Of the free heavens? Come now, think of it
As the usual dipping of day's flag. You used
To love this room at night.

ROSABEL. How do you know?
How can you tell who loves, or when or why they love,
You without a single beat of heart
Worth measuring? You sit up here all night
Looking at the stars, travelling farther and farther
Away from living people. I hate your telescope!
How can you know, and what, if you knew, can it mean,
What can the darkest bruise on the human mind
Mean, when nothing beats against you heavier
Than a fall of rain? And out you whip
Your impervious umbrella of satisfaction!
How you prink across every puddle, and laugh
To think that other men can drown.
You would never believe there are some affections
Which would rather have decent burial
Than this mocking perpetuation you offer them.
You're a devil, a devil, a devil, a devil!

DUKE. Only
On one side of the family, Rosabel,
Please believe that.

431

EDGAR [*taking the apple from her hand*].
I beg your pardon; I think
I've made a mistake.

ROSABEL. Now I must go. I've spoilt
The eclipse. For that I'm sorry.

DUKE. It's frankly impossible
To spoil the eclipse.

REEDBECK. It would be fanciful
No doubt to say that the moon has placed a penny
Not on the dead but on the living eye of the sun.

EDGAR. Yes, Reedbeck, it would.

[21]

JESSIE. Don't you be put down.
It's nice that anyone can say anything at all.

DUKE. So Rosabel believes when the cold spell comes
And we're compelled to enter this draughty time
And shuffle about in the slipshod leaves,
Leaves disbanded, leaves at a loose end,
And we know we're in for the drifting of the fall,
We should merely shiver and be silent: never speak
Of the climate of Eden, or the really magnificent
Foliage of the tree of knowledge,
Or the unforgettable hushed emerald
Of the coiling and fettering serpent:
Pretend we never knew it, because love
Quite naturally condescended
To the passing of time. But why should we, Rosabel?

HILDA. But if what I gather to be true is true,
Though it's no business of mine,
I must say, Hereward, you certainly seem to have been
Coruscating on thin ice. I think
She has cause to be angry. I do think so.
You've behaved a great deal less than well.

DUKE. I've behaved according to my lights of love
Which were excellent and bright and much to be
Remembered. You have all of you been my moments
Of revelation. I wish I understood why
You want to behave like skeletons in my cupboard.

JESSIE. Not Jessie, alas; her weight is all against it.
But need we make Miss Fleming cry?

EDGAR. I'd like it,
Father, if Mrs. Dill would have this apple.

JESSIE. I'd like it, too; though it's prettier on the tree.

ROSABEL. Your moments of revelation! I only wonder
What we revealed. Certainly not
What goes on in other hearts than your own.
That's as remote to you as a seaside lodging-house
To a passing whale.

HILDA.   Could she put it more fairly?

JESSIE. I remember seeing what was thought to be a whale
At somewhere like Tenby; at least, my father said
Look, there's a whale, Jessie; but all I saw
Was the tip of a fin which might have been finnan haddy
Or Father Neptune or an old forgotten
Channel swimmer.

REEDBECK.   Can you play with Leviathan
As with a bird? That's really quite the strangest
Of rhetorical questions. And when will my daughter come?

DUKE. Rosabel——

JESSIE.   We might as well never have changed the subject.

DUKE. Rosabel, why pick on me to be
The villain? I'm a Roman in a world
Of Romans, and all creation can recognize me
As genus Man. Old men, young men, virgins,
Viragoes, all walk hand in hand with me
In the green enclosure of insensibility.
An individual torment in Indo-China
Makes less noise in your ear than the drop of a fir cone.
So why do I have to be sensible
Of a heart which is fortunate enough to be
Four thousand miles nearer my way, someone,
Moreover, to whom I've already given pleasure
And the refuge of a bed, which I never gave
(Such is my frailty) to the Indo-Chinee?

[23]

Don't let's go mad with inconsistency.
Either everything shall be near, or everything
Shall be far. Allow me the wrong end of the telescope;
I like to conform.

JESSIE.   Mr. Reedbeck will propose
The vote of thanks.

REEDBECK.   I really think, a few moments ago,
I heard what could only have been a motor-car.

ROSABEL. Where have I got myself now? Into such
An embarrassment, if I could vanish I should vanish,
And even then transparently kick myself.
It was hopelessly stupid.

HILDA.   Stupid, and what was called,
In the days when musk had a scent, indelicate.

DUKE. I shall plough up the orchard, Edgar;
It was never a great success.

> [*The shadow lifts from the sun, and the light falls on*
> PERPETUA REEDBECK.

EDGAR.   God be praised,
The sun again.

REEDBECK.   My daughter, it's my daughter, Perpetua,
My dear, my dear!

> [PERPETUA *runs to him.*

ROSABEL.   Where shall I hide a most
Unhappy head?

> [*Exit* ROSABEL.

REEDBECK.   O my little sixpenny
Ha'penny daughter, home again, home again,
Home again!

[24]

HILDA [*thinking of* ROSABEL].
Can she take care of herself, that woman?
[*She follows* ROSABEL.

PERPETUA. Let me look at you. Every feature where I left it
Ten years ago! I'd forgotten you were so beautiful.

REEDBECK. You mustn't spoil me, not so soon;
I shall puff myself up and explode like a frog.

PERPETUA. Perhaps we should sing until we're used to it?
Might that be the wise thing?

REEDBECK.   I should stop at every
Note to listen to you. But, my dear,
I must present you to his Grace. I'd forgotten
We were not in heaven. Your Grace—this—
This is——

DUKE.   Steady, Reedbeck.
Let me dry your eyes. Dear man, these tears are something
Remarkably like champagne.

REEDBECK.   No doubt they are.
My dear daughter: his Grace the Duke of Altair.

DUKE. You have made your father as happy as if his heart
Were breaking. And isn't it likely you're going to make
Others happy as well? We have only autumn
To offer you, England's moist and misty devotion,
But spring may come in time to reconcile you
If you'll wait so long.

PERPETUA.   I need no reconciling.
I was born and grew in this green and pleasant aquarium,
And I've spent four days on a wicked October sea
For love of recollected mildew
And my dear frog-father; only I'd scarcely expected
Quite so much impenetrable murk

[25]

In the middle of morning. Surely there must be something
Out of sorts about your daylight?

DUKE.   Nothing
Which time won't mend. But, first, let me introduce—
Ah, they've left us; Hilda and Rosabel
Have passed away with no last word. They always
Bore themselves with the true brevity of empires.
But here is Mrs. Dill, more universe
Than empire, less conquered but more embracing.

JESSIE. I'm very pleased to meet you. Your father loves you
With every word in the language.

DUKE.   And this, Miss Reedbeck,
Is my first youth, my younger days: The Marquis
Of Charlock.

EDGAR.   You're a kind of legend with us here,
But the truth is better.

PERPETUA.   I'll tell you the truth:
I'm very happy this morning; I'm really out
Of prison.

REEDBECK. Of prison, my darling? Why do you say
Of prison?

PERPETUA. I mean, of course, the boat was a prison
And the frowning sea was Dartmoor.

DUKE.   To refresh you
There's wine in the bottle, cider from the wood,
Biscuits in the barrel; and there you can see
Our English sun, convalescent after passing
Through the valley of the shadow of the moon.

PERPETUA. So that was why I had to search my way
Up the stairs in gloom. How far off is the sun?

DUKE. The best part of ninety-three million miles.

PERPETUA. You would hardly think it could matter.

EDGAR.   What will you
   drink,
 Miss Reedbeck?

PERPETUA.   Something of England, the cider, presently.
 I'm so at peace, though I still can feel
 The lunge of the sea. Your floor isn't meant to sway?

DUKE. The floor is battering at your feet like Attila
 With a horde of corybantic atoms,
 And travelling at eighteen miles a second,
 But it cannot be said to sway.

JESSIE.   That would be much
 Too easy.

DUKE.   Our stability is a matter
 For surprise.

REEDBECK.   I feel the terrible truth of that.
 Even now, for example, when I see my Perpetua
 Sitting like a girl on a swing on an Easter Monday
 Under a Wedgwood sky, I can feel my heart——

PERPETUA. That's just what it's like, a girl on a swing.

REEDBECK.   My heart
 Knocking most anxiously against the future,
 As though afraid to be alone with the present time:
 Ready, really, for almost any disaster
 Rather than this unsteady tight-rope of joy
 I'm walking on now. Are you ill, perhaps? Is that it?
 Have you come home for your health?

PERPETUA.   I've come home to be home.
 A pigeon's return—just so simple, Poppadillo.

[27]

I wanted to stand where I first grew, and to have
My roots and my branches all in one place together.
And that's no curious thing. Here, swinging
On my swing, with the Atlantic foam still racing
Under my eyelids, I seem at rest already.
And so I sent no word to say I was coming,
Because, in the sense that means the most,
I was here all the time.

EDGAR.   And so you emerged
Like Venus from the sea.

PERPETUA.   But sicker.

REEDBECK.   What
Shall I do for my returning Mayflower
Suppose she is disappointed in the land
Her roots are in?

PERPETUA.   You needn't be afraid.
If this is still an island
Enclosed in a druid circle of stony sea,
As misty as it was that chilly Thursday
When I was born to the wilting of plovers
And the smell of a saturation of hops,
Then I'm safely and happily home.

JESSIE.   Here's to your happiness,
Dear; God save the King, and a mild winter.

REEDBECK. Your happiness, my dear.

EDGAR.   Happiness, Miss Reedbeck.

DUKE. I should like you to offer Miss Reedbeck an apple, Edgar.

EDGAR. Anything except an apple, father.
I will offer her
The cloudy peach, the bristling pineapple,

[28]

The dropsical pear, the sportive orange,
Apricot, sloe, King William, or a carillon
Of grapes, but not, as God's my judge, an apple.

DUKE. Then, as Paris abdicates, I must offer
The sweet round robin fruit myself—

> [*He holds an apple up between his fingers.*

The green sphere the myth of the world began in,
Which Melanion let fall, delaying
Mercurial Atalanta—

> [PERPETUA *has whipped a very small pistol from a pig-skin
> holster at her belt. She shoots and shatters the apple. There
> is an incredulous, shaken silence.*

PERPETUA. I—I'm terribly sorry. That was thoughtless of me.
Perhaps you wanted to eat it.

DUKE.   There are others;
Nature is pleased to give us more. And you
Have been very good; you let me keep my fingers.

REEDBECK. Only by the mercy of God! My dear girl,
My dear girl! What in the world possessed you?
You might have been the death of him!

PERPETUA.   No, it was quite safe.
To please, I always aim. But that, I agree,
Is no excuse. It was dreadful, and shameful of me.
I was thinking of something else, or else
It would never have happened.

Enter ROSABEL, *followed by* HILDA.

ROSABEL.   What was it? We heard a sound
Like a shot!

REEDBECK.   Good gracious, a *sound* like a shot!

HILDA. Is no one hurt?

DUKE.   An apple came to grief
As apples must.

EDGAR.   One pip too many.

JESSIE.   And nobody
Was more surprised than the Duke.

REEDBECK.   Oh, yes, I think so,
I think my surprise can hardly have been bettered
Except, no doubt, by the apple. And I'm still
Anchored in amazement, I have to confess.

PERPETUA. I also have to confess; I see I must.
I thought I could come back again to England
And slip into this new beginning, silently.
But now the pistol has gone off; the silence anyway
Is well and truly broken, and so I'll explain,
Though the explanation, I'm afraid, will seem
As wild as the shot.

REEDBECK.   What can it be? Be quick
And tell me.

PERPETUA.   I've lately been in prison. But not
For what we should call a crime.

REEDBECK.   They put you in prison
Without rhyme or reason?

PERPETUA.   There may have been
A little rhyme. I was thought to be unsafe
For democracy, because I broke, or shot,
Or burnt, a good many things, or rather—and this
Is the reason—a bad many things: the unsightly,
The gimcrack, the tedious, the hideous, the spurious,
The harmful. Not I alone, of course;
We were all students, and called ourselves

[30]

The Society for the Desecration
Of Ancient and Modern Monumental Errors.
We destroyed, or tried to destroy, whatever we loathed
As bad.

ROSABEL. Whatever you loathed, you destroyed?
Why, that was admirable, superb, the most
Heavenly daring!

PERPETUA.   No, I think it was only
Exasperation. And then we went to prison.
And there I knew it was all no use.
The more we destroyed, the worse the bad sprang up.
And I thought and thought, What can I do for the world?
I was wearing the prison drab. My name was a number.
Inside or outside the prison, Perpetua
(I thought), you're no one, you're everybody's colour.
You must make good, before you break the bad,
Perpetua. And so I came home to England
Simply to trace myself, in my own way.

                    [*She offers the pistol to the* DUKE.

I'd better surrender this. I only kept it
For a kind of memento. And I apologize
Again for destroying the apple. Still half at sea
As I am, it appeared to be, in a misty way,
Like a threat to my new-come freedom.

DUKE. I hope you will think so again, some other time.

ROSABEL [*taking the pistol*]. May I have it, to remind me of your
    story,
To know there has been someone in the world
Who dared to do such things! If only I
Could be such a brave one, there might be
Some justification for me.

[31]

DUKE [*taking it from her*].   Caps for you,
   Dear Rosabel, not bullets. I'll have it
   Filled for your next big scene.

                              [*A gong booms from below.*

EDGAR. Luncheon! Can we be supposed to eat
   On a day when the sun is drowned by the moon,
   And apples meet such a strange end?

DUKE. I see nothing strange. If we can move and talk
   Under the sun at all, we must have accepted
   The incredible as commonplace, long ago;
   And even the incredible must eat.
   Shall we go down?

               THE CURTAIN FALLS ON ACT ONE

ACT TWO

SCENE ONE

The Temple of the Ancient Virtues, beside the ducal lake, in the afternoon. DOMINIC *and* PERPETUA *are there.*

DOMINIC. You haven't spoken for three and a half minutes.

———

Four minutes. This is the most pregnant pause
Since darkness was on the face of the deep. I suppose
You think I shouldn't have told you.

PERPETUA. Oh, yes, you should.

DOMINIC. It was better than leaving you in a fool's paradise,
You must admit.

PERPETUA. I could be twice as silent
For seven times as long.

DOMINIC. Well, then you shall be.
I know myself how the shock stuns one.

PERPETUA. No shock
At all. I was able to believe you at once.
Poppadillo has the most beguiling
Jackdaw look about him. But you think
He wouldn't be happy in prison?

DOMINIC. He wouldn't, but what
Difference does that make? Would you be able
To look anyone in the face, with a father jailed?

[33]

PERPETUA. Oh, yes, if he were comfortable. But I think
He might feel shut in. No, Dominic, I'm sure
You're right. If someone has to go to prison,
· I must.

DOMINIC. You? What can you possibly mean?

PERPETUA. You said I should have to, and now all I mean
Is Yes, quite so.

DOMINIC.   Quite what is quite so, will you tell me?

PERPETUA. I heard you say, perhaps it might have been
Six minutes ago, if I made myself agreeable
The Duke (you said) being much in that mind at the moment
Might, with any luck, be inclined to marry me,
And no gentleman (you added) would incriminate
His father-in-law. And I agree with you,
And I see my carefree hours already numbered,
My freedom of choice and my individual day.
I'm no longer a woman after my own heart.
Broad cupid's arrows on my wedding veil.
But still, Dominic, for my father's sake
Not ours, I mean to try.

DOMINIC.   God bless you, then,
And God speed you, and thank God I can breathe again.
And a coronet's no martyrdom, particularly
When it sits on a man whom women find easy to like.

PERPETUA. I wonder how many women have stood perplexed
And plagued in this temple, two whole centuries of them,
Looking out this way, on the same view
Of the metal rusting year. Lemon, amber,
Umber, bronze and brass, oxblood, damson,
Crimson, scalding scarlet, black cedar,
And the willow's yellow fall to grace.

[34]

DOMINIC. Do you have to be so melancholy? Everything
Is better now. Though there is still the anxiety
Whether you can prepossess him before he strikes.

PERPETUA. Oh, yes, there is that anxiety still.
Here comes the straying lamb who gave us life.

DOMINIC. Don't pamper him. We have to make him realize
He's been sinning all this while.

PERPETUA.   He looks as worried
As though he knew it already.

                Enter REEDBECK, *out of breath.*

REEDBECK.   So here—here—
You are. I wondered, missed you, but luckily caught
Sight of you going down through the trees. I lost
My hat on the way; it blew (oh, what a gasping old fellow)
Off, blew off; now upside down on the water
Among the *Alisma Plantago-aquatica.*
Didn't think I should have enough breath to say so.

PERPETUA. Try only breathing, for a time; that's always
Nice.

DOMINIC. What was the hurry? Did you think I was going
To throw her in the water?

REEDDECK.   Among the *Alisma
Plantago-aquatica.* Has he been talking to you?
He's not as fond of me as either of us
Would like.

PERPETUA.   I've been hearing unimaginable
Things about you.

REEDBECK.   Yes, the imagination
Is a frail craft, soon capsizes, quite understand.
Now this, my dear, called sometimes the Temple
Of the Ancient Virtues, and at other times

[35]

The White Temple, both because it is white
And because it was designed by Martin White
In seventeen hundred and ninety-three, was erected
By the third Duke of Altair for his wife Claire
For her use when she played the part of the Delphic Oracle,
A way she had of informing the Duke of her pregnancy,
Which she did on twenty-seven separate occasions.

PERPETUA. Tell me why you've been cheating the Duke,
There's a good boy. What made you do it?

REEDBECK.   I hope
I've done nothing so monosyllabic as to cheat.
A spade is never so merely a spade as the word
Spade would imply.

DOMINIC.   One's helpless to help him.

PERPETUA. Poppadillo, suppose I put it this way:
What made you supercherify with chousery
The Duke?

REEDBECK.   That might be said to—that perhaps
Is not an unfair expression. And I say in reply
The reason was the fading charm of the world.
The banquet of civilization is over——

PERPETUA.   Shall we call it
The groaning board?

REEDBECK.   You may call it what you will.
With a little wealth to do it I should like to perform
The grace after the meat, a last, gentlemanly,
Valedictory grace: a grace for departing grace
(Is that not rather good?):
The spacious lawns of life are being
Inevitably ploughed, and we don't know, we really
Don't know, what's going to be sown there.

[36]

Dignity has dropped upon all fours.
Indeed there's hardly to be seen
One intense perpendicular
In all the streets of men. Someone, you know,
Someone must keep alive that quality
Of living which separates us from the brutes;
And I have proposed it should be I.

DOMINIC. It should be me.

REEDBECK.   Beloved boy,
It would be delightful if you thought so.

PERPETUA. I understand so far; I only wonder
Why the Duke has to be . . . out of pocket.

REEDBECK. I care so much for civilization,
Its patrician charm, its grave nobility;
He cares so little. Therefore certain eccentric
Means have had to be taken for splendid ends.
Church and State, in a way, agree
In justifying such a course of action.
A kind of casual taxation. I hope I explain
Quite clearly. It's true I have overlaid the Law
With a certain transposition; we might
Call this process Reedbequity. But what
A gain to the world.

DOMINIC.   Do you hear that, Perpetua?
He even unblushingly gives our name
To his wicked practices!

PERPETUA.   Dominic wants us all
To be good. Perhaps if you had gone to the Duke
And explained all this, he would have eased the path
To Reedbequity without the bother of iniquity.
Don't you think he might?

[37]

REEDBECK. My dear, I've never believed
In the equal distribution of property.
I only think it can have more beauty
In my hands than in his. But that would have been
A most impertinent thing to say to him.

PERPETUA. We must keep you from harm. Heydee,
I'm not to be myself, I see.
I'm sad to see myself go;
But I was only promise, after all,
And the world can't live on that.

REEDBECK. Have you something that worries you? I believe
I've made you discontented with me, on a day
Which should have turned out so glorious, and now
I don't know *where* we are.

DOMINIC. It's only a step
From where you are, father, to where you will be
If we can't prevent it. You'll discover
Civilization is sadly dwindled when
You make your way to prison. Here's the Duke.
Be cheerful, if you can, Perpetua.

PERPETUA. My smile
Will be like the glint of handcuffs, but he's very
Welcome to it. Sing out a joke, Dominic,
In your merry way.

DOMINIC. Ssh!

PERPETUA. That's a most promising
Start to a conversation. There must be a joke
Lying about somewhere, even when the leaves are falling.

REEDBECK. Something about . . . when the leaves in Eden fell . . .

PERPETUA. Dear Poppadillo; thank you.

[38]

REEDBECK.   Was it at all
  Serviceable?

PERPETUA.   It had a kind of ancient virtue,
  Proper for this time and temple, yes.

        Enter the DUKE, *carrying a bow and quiver.*

DUKE. May your little girl come out and play, Reedbeck?
  Daylight is short, and becoming always shorter.
  But there's the space for an arrow or two between
  Now and the sunset.

PERPETUA.   I've never handled a bow.
  How shall I manage?

DUKE.   Beautifully.
  The light will hang fire to see you; you might
  Even hear the flash of the foliage
  Where Artemis parts the leaves to patronize
  And praise you; but take no notice, and watch what you're doing,
  And do what I tell you.

PERPETUA.   Implicitly.

DUKE.   Take notice
  Of the excellent marksmanship of the year, whose arrow
  Singing from the April bow crossed over the width
  Of summer straight for the gold, where now, if you look,
  You will see it quivering.

PERPETUA.   The year has a world of experience.
  But still, show me; and I'll try not to shame the shades
  Of all the arching duchesses and ladies
  Who played on these lawns before.

DUKE.   They'll arch the more,
  Adoring what you do, feathering their shafts
  And shooting until doomsday's Parthian shot.

                        [39]

Be confident; and, if you miss,
The fashion of the game will be to miss,
Until you change your mind and hit.

> [*He begins to instruct her in the use of the bow, holding it with
> her, and speaking low into her ear, so that* REEDBECK *and*
> DOMINIC *cannot hear.*

And then, Perpetua, to-night
If a clear sky inclines you to it, and the heavens
Remain suspended, how would it be
If we trained the telescope on the infinite
And made what we could of what we could see of it?
Are you still as interested as you were
This morning?

PERPETUA.   Yes. I come from a city. The stars
Are new to me.

DUKE.   They shall answer you
By numbers. But we'll not tell the world
What we mean to do. There's a little tension to-day
Already, nerves perhaps not ready to accept
The quiet session of scientific study
You and I propose. So let's be as mute
As we're mutable, and avoid misapprehension.

PERPETUA. I—if so—if so—yes, very well.

DUKE. You can tell the world you need a long night of sleep.

PERPETUA. Yes, yes, I can. But here's the good afternoon light
Fading to waste unless we make use of it.

DUKE. I know that thought so well. Come on, then,
Let the trial begin.

PERPETUA.   Watch me, Poppadillo.
Come and judge what a huntress I should make,

[40]

What a rival for Artemis, and what chance Actaeon
Would have if I pursued him.

[*Exeunt the* DUKE *and* PERPETUA.

REEDBECK.   She really makes me
Respectful of astrology; it must
Have been the arrangement of stars she was born under.
It couldn't have been all me and her mother. Why,
I couldn't even dream so beautifully,
Let alone propagate. It must have been
The state of the zodiac when she was conceived.
But even so, I was there, and that in itself
Is remarkable. What did you say to her, Dominic;
What did you say to her?

DOMINIC.   I simply told her
You were crooked.

REEDBECK.   And then she said?

DOMINIC.   She said
She was not surprised.

REEDBECK.   Oh. *I* should have been;
It would have seemed like a thunder clap to *me*.
But you've made her feel differently towards me,
You've sent me off on my own again. And what
Did she mean by 'sad to see herself go', and 'not
To be herself any more'? What made her say that?
Was something agreed between you?

DOMINIC.   I made a point.

REEDBECK. What point, now what point?

DOMINIC.   I made the suggestion
She might like to marry the Duke, and save you that way.

REEDBECK. You—said—such a—thing? You dared

[41]

To consider selling your sister? You,
Sprung from my loins, and so utterly
Unprincipled?

DOMINIC.   That sounds most convincing,
Coming from you!

REEDBECK.   Poor little girl, poor
Little girl. But I'll intervene—*inter venio*,
Yes—though I can't relieve her
Of her inhuman brother.

DOMINIC.   Or her dishonest
Father.

REEDBECK [*shaking him, in a sudden burst of rage*]. You're a vain,
    vexing, incomprehensible,
Crimping, constipated duffer. What's your heart?
All plum duff! Why do I have to be
So inarticulate? God give me a few
Lithontriptical words! You grovelling little
Gobemouche!

DOMINIC.   Stop it, father, stop it at once!

REEDBECK. You spigoted, bigoted, operculated prig!

Enter JESSIE.

JESSIE. Am I in the way? I came to write a letter.

        [REEDBECK *releases* DOMINIC *suddenly, and* DOMINIC
        trips and falls sprawling on the floor.

REEDBECK. I was having a word with my son.

JESSIE [*to* DOMINIC].   How do you do?
Please don't bother to get up.

REEDBECK.   You're very welcome
To write your letter. I don't wish to shake him

[42]

Any more. But if you hadn't come in
I think I should have gone on shaking him
Until I couldn't see him.

JESSIE.   He would still
Have been there, of course. When my mother used to shake me
It always gave me hiccups, and then I was given
Peppermint on sugar to cure them. If only your son
Had hiccups, and you had peppermint and sugar,
Mr. Reedbeck, everything would seem different.

DOMINIC. I have to leave you. I'm afraid my father
Must be feeling very chastened and confused.

[*Exit* DOMINIC.

JESSIE. It was lovely exercise for both of you.

REEDBECK. It did no good; I've only shaken my own
Composure.

JESSIE.   Sit down, Mr. Reedbeck, and let it settle.
I have to get a few lines off every day
To my father, eighty-seven. He can't read a word
Of my handwriting, and doesn't try, but he likes
The postman.

REEDBECK.   Well, I'll leave you, then;
I won't stop and hinder you. I suppose
That action of mine, that sudden accession of rage,
Wasn't in the nicest mood of civilization?
And yet I don't at all feel like apologizing,
I don't feel at all like apologizing. Would you apologize?

JESSIE. I'm sorry, I was trying to think how to begin
So that Dad won't mind he can't read it.

REEDBECK. Well, I won't stop and hinder you now,
But I should be very upset if I proved to be
Nothing but a barbarian after all,

[43]

A barbarian dreaming of the higher excellences.
But I won't stop and hinder you.

Enter HILDA.

                           Mrs. Dill
Is trying to write a letter. We mustn't hinder her.

                                    [*Exit* REEDBECK.

HILDA. I see Hereward has made another backward
   Flight into his heyday. It's a handsome thing
   To see him so happy, but are we so happy for the girl?

JESSIE. Doesn't she like playing at bows and arrows?

HILDA. She does, no doubt, but—May I interrupt you?

JESSIE.   I'm only
   Writing a letter when nothing else occurs to me;
   I like to talk.

HILDA.   Because of the strange business
   Of the eclipse this morning, and what went on,
   We've been thrown into each other's confidence
   Unexpectedly soon. And for my part
   I think I'm thankful. I've always hidden more
   Than was good for me, hoping in that way
   To make my life seem pleasant to everyone,
   But who should care? So I've lost the habit
   Of daring to ask myself what I do, or why.
   Why did I come here to-day, and what did I expect?
   And why did he ever invite us here together?
   I know him painstakingly enough
   To be sure it was kindly meant; it couldn't have been
   To watch our faces fall.

JESSIE.   I like being here
   So much I never even wondered.

HILDA. There
    Was still something in me to be hurt,
    Which a little surprised me. And then
    Reedbeck's daughter came, as though to show
    How the years had gone by for us
    But not for him, as though the old
    Magician in his blood was bound to draw us
    Into that revealing circle. But I sigh
    For her, as once I sighed for myself; and, if
    I knew how, I should tell her how lightly he flies.

JESSIE. And then
    You must tell her how nicely he alights.
    That's important, too.
    I should let them be, because be they will.

HILDA. When I first met him, I remember, he seemed
    At once to give my spirits a holiday,
    Though (like a first holiday abroad) almost too unlike
    The daily round of the roundabout life I led—
    And lead still, O my heavens—which had, and has,
    All the appearance of movement without covering
    Any ground whatsoever. I know I have
    No particular heights or depths myself;
    No one who thought me ordinary or dull
    Would be far wrong. But even I despair
    For Roderic, my husband, who really is
    The height of depth, if it doesn't sound unkind
    To say so: not deep depth, but a level depth
    Of dullness. Once he had worn away the sheen
    Of his quite becoming boyhood, which made me fancy him,
    There was nothing to be seen in Roderic
    For mile after mile after mile, except
    A few sheeplike thoughts nibbling through the pages

Of a shiny weekly, any number of dead pheasants,
Partridges, pigeons, jays, and hares,
An occasional signpost of extreme prejudice
Marked 'No thoroughfare', and the flat horizon
Which is not so much an horizon
As a straight ruled line beyond which one doesn't look.

JESSIE. Keep him warm and fed. They bloom
Once in seven years.

HILDA.   Not Roderic.

Enter EDGAR, *carrying a bow and quiver.*

EDGAR. Are either of you ladies any good
At taking out a thorn? I took a look
In a mirror for some reason or other, and there it was.
A bramble slashed me when I was out riding yesterday.
I've brought my own needle.

HILDA.   Am I hurting you?

EDGAR. Yes, but how nice of you. Isn't it strange?
For the first time in my young life
I'm jealous of my father. I thought I'd better
Mention it before I begin to brood.

HILDA. Jealous of him, why?

EDGAR.   To me he's a man
Once and for all; once, once only,
And certainly for all. And any man
Who has to follow him (me, for instance)
Feels like the lag-last in a cloud of locusts:
By the time I come to a tree it's as bare
As a hat stand. Talent, conversation, wit,
Ease, and friendliness are all swallowed up
In advance. And just at present
I feel depressed about it.

[46]

HILDA.   Now, take heart.
　　You have those virtues, too. There's room for both of you.

EDGAR. Not, I think, at the moment.

JESSIE.   Do you mean
　　Only two can play at bows and arrows?

HILDA. I think at the moment it's greatly important
　　There *should* be room for both of you. Suppose
　　You make a bid for it. Why not?
　　Nothing hinders you except weakness of hope,
　　And that's ridiculous. We'll go together.
　　Mrs. Dill wants to write a letter.

JESSIE.   Never mind;
　　Everything writes itself in time.

Enter BATES.

BATES. It's Mrs. Taylor-Snell I'm looking for;
　　Oh, that's right, lady, you're here. I have
　　A message to give you, they said; prompto.
　　On the telephone it come. It's not so nice
　　As you might like to have it, but it's not so bad.
　　It seems there's been a bit of a accident,
　　And they'd be glad if you could make it convenient
　　To find your way back 'ome.

HILDA.   Roderic!

BATES. Whoever it is, missis, you're not to worry.
　　Your old man has got hisself throwed off his horse,
　　Hunting little rabbits and uvver breeders.
　　Now, now, lady, you never know,
　　It may only be a front toof a bit loose.

HILDA. Didn't they say what the injury was?

[47]

BATES. Took a bit of a toss, come a bit of a purler,
   What Jack and Jill done; don't you worry, lady.

HILDA. I can't help worrying, dear Bates. [*To* JESSIE] I'll go
   Without saying good-bye to Hereward. There's no reason
   Why anyone's afternoon should suffer,
   Except mine; and later I'll telephone
   And tell you what has happened.

JESSIE.   It's wretched for you,
   It's really wretched for you; I'm awfully sorry.
   What would you like me to do?

HILDA.   Nothing, except
   To forget I laughed at him. I have my car;
   I can slip away easily.

EDGAR.   I'll run on ahead
   And get the car started for you.

HILDA.   No.
   Thank you, but I'd rather go quietly alone.
   If you want to do something for me, put your shoulders
   To your father, and make yourself your own success.
   Good-bye.

EDGAR.   Good-bye, good luck.

JESSIE.   I expect you'll find
   It's something nice and simple like a collar-bone.
                                        [*Exit* HILDA.
   Oh, please God, make it a collar-bone. She turned
   So pale and unhappy, poor lamb.

BATES. I wouldn't have anything happen to that one:
   It's a pity we can't do something to oblige her.
   But there's that uvver one, Fleming she says she's called:
   Flaming nuisance, I reply: what about her,
   Eh, miss? What's she doing snooping

[48]

About the east wing all the afternoon? I tell you,
Miss, I knows an undesirable character
When I see one; I've been one myself for years.

JESSIE. And look how we love you. So don't you have
Nasty thoughts about Miss Fleming, who is not
Undesirable at all. And go away
Like a good boy, and let me write my letter.

BATES. I just fought you might like the opinion of a expert.

[*He begins wandering away.*

But don't let's say anyfing good about
Captain Fussing Reddleman, lord of the kitchens.
He can go and tame his lions on some uvver poor bastard's mug.
I prefers to keep mine natural.

[*Exit* BATES.

EDGAR. I wonder if I should.

JESSIE.   If you should what?

EDGAR. From here I think I could send an arrow right past him
Into the target.

JESSIE.   If you think you can, then do.

[EDGAR *takes an arrow, fits it in his bow, and shoots. A
distant cry of remonstrance from the* DUKE.

EDGAR. Oh, that was very beautiful. I enjoyed that
Extremely.

JESSIE.   What did you do? Did I encourage you
To be mischievous? I was thinking about my letter.
You might have shot your father.

EDGAR.   I jolly nearly
Did. But my arrows, I never quite know why,
Have a considerate way of going where
I mean them to go, which was nearer the gold than his.
He's probably shooting not so well

[49]

To give Perpetua some encouragement.
When I come to think of it, that shot of mine
Was taking a very easy advantage.

JESSIE. I shouldn't say easy, twice the distance off.
And as you didn't kill anybody, I may say
I think it was splendid, and I think perhaps
You should do it more often.

Enter the DUKE.

DUKE. What, by Saint Sebastian's groin,
Do you think you're up to? Edgar, for goodness' sake!

EDGAR. I was drawing a bow at a venture, father.

DUKE.   So
I thought. But remember what damage was done to Sir Lancelot
By an arrow in the buttocks. Did I beget you
To be shot from behind?

EDGAR.   I'm extremely sorry,
But you took a step to the south.

DUKE.   Am I never to move?

EDGAR. Oh, yes, father, but the other way, or any way
Except between me and where I aim.

DUKE.   I hope
I'm being patient. I had quite supposed
The contest was between Miss Reedbeck and me.

EDGAR. When all the time it was really between you
And your loving son; or so my hackles tell me.

DUKE. Ah—! Now I see;
Your days are starting to press upon me,
You who were always so unassuming and easy.
But not this time. No, I'm sorry,
Not this time, Edgar.

[50]

EDGAR. It is this time.
I'm sorry, too, but it is this time. You've had
A long innings, and a summer of splendid outings,
And now I must ask you, father, not to monopolize
Every heart in the world any longer.

JESSIE. Excuse me
Worrying you, but how do you spell epidemic?
Two *p*'s and two *m*'s?

EDGAR. I'd forgotten we weren't alone.

DUKE. We're alone with Jessie; nothing could be happier.
One *p*, one *m*. If the generations join
In a life-and-death struggle under your feet
Don't let it, Jessie, disturb your spelling.

JESSIE. One *p*, one *m*. Quite enough, when you look at it.

DUKE. Now listen, Edgar, take nothing for granted,
Not even my flair for breaking into love;
You're apprehensive far too soon. The field,
If not entirely yours, is not entirely mine:
I am as innocently there
As an old warhorse put out to grass:
My equine equability is pastoral to a fault.

EDGAR. But when you're grazing you're irresistible;
Buttercups and daisies fall to your fetlocks in swathes;
I've seen it happen. And between this morning's eclipse
And this afternoon you've lost the autumnal look
Which was such a comfort to me; I see you have
The appearance of a very mild March day.
And what does a boy do then?

DUKE. Aren't you being
Just a thought parricidal for a fine afternoon?

[51]

EDGAR. Oh, God, I love you like the rest of them.
　　I'm only asking you to forgo yourself
　　This once, to suspend your animation
　　For a few short months, for my sake.

DUKE.　　　　　　　　　　　　　Edgar,
　　I mean to be a good father to you, but
　　A good father must be a man. And what
　　Is a man? Edgar, what is a man? O
　　My man-child, what in the world is a man?
　　Speaking for myself, I am precisely that question:
　　I exist to know that I exist
　　Interrogatively. But what gives birth
　　To a question? A desire to be answered. A question
　　Desires, as a man must desire, as I
　　Desire. That, at least, you'll allow me.
　　You wouldn't have your father merely rhetorical.

EDGAR. Not at all, but——

DUKE.　　　　　　　　But what is the mark of the question?
　　What is the note of this interrogation?
　　Loneliness. The note, my son, is loneliness.
　　Over all the world
　　Men move unhoming, and eternally
　　Concerned: a swarm of bees who have lost their queen.
　　Nothing else is so ill at ease. We know
　　How patiently the toad suns on the stone,
　　How the indolent fish waves its tail in time
　　With the waving weed. If a pulse was in the stone,
　　And the stone grew moist, and the toad petrified,
　　Patience would still be as patient in the sun.
　　Or if the weed wove its way up river
　　To breed, and the fish waved green and still,
　　The water would never wonder: all

[52]

Is at one with the rest.
And the trees, when the weather is waking, quicken without
Question, their leaves assemble in a perfect faith
Of summer; and so with all the world's life,
Except ours. We can hear the lyric lark
Flaking its limit of heaven from a cloud,
And see the self-assimilated cat,
The adaptable chameleon, and the mole
Rubbing along companionably
With the obliging earth. But where, O Edgar,
Is an element compatible with *us*?

EDGAR. Would you mind if I reminded you, father,
What we were talking about when you started talking?

DUKE. Thank you, but I know: your wish to remove me.
But if being alive is a question, heaven-bent
For an answer, and the question is a man's
Estrangement in a world
Where everything else conforms, how should I dare
To suspend myself for a day, or even an hour,
When that hour might ravish me
Into a complete, unsolitary life,
Where happiness leaves no room for the restless mind
And I, as unlaborious
As a laburnum tree, hang in caresses of gold.

EDGAR. And what do I hang in?

DUKE.   You hang in abeyance, Edgar.
If I should die, with the great question unanswered,
I leave myself in you to ask it still.
But this is all academic. The field is still open.

JESSIE. I always think 'niece' is such a difficult word.

DUKE. *I* before *E*, except after *C*. And so,
Edgar, let nothing dismay you——

JESSIE.   Except
   In the case of 'neigh', that humorous noise of a horse.

Enter PERPETUA.

PERPETUA. Is archery all over? I went to the lake
   And tried to spear fish with an arrow, but I'm tired
   Of that.

DUKE.   Edgar, I'm nowhere to be seen;
   For all the personality I exert
   You might never have had a father; advance, advance,
   You son of a cipher.

PERPETUA.   Could we not all shoot together?

EDGAR. Miss Reedbeck——

PERPETUA.   Perpetua.

EDGAR.   Yes. Perpetua,
   This is All Hallowe'en. To-night half England
   Will be dancing in memory of a world they don't remember.
   The sky will very likely be black with broomsticks.
   There's a dance on in the Old Woolmarket
   At Mordenbury. Will you come?

PERPETUA [*glancing towards the* DUKE]. All Hallowe'en.
   I should have liked it dearly, but to-night——

EDGAR. You've made some other plan.

PERPETUA.   No, no.

EDGAR. Then come. Meet England first among the wisps
   Of magic we still possess. Will you, Perpetua?

PERPETUA. If I dared to trust my eyes and my feet
   To be lively, so long after sunset,
   I should say yes willingly. But I must and will
   Sleep early. Four days on the see-saw sea,

[54]

And then such a wave of homecoming, have left me
Ready to rest. I'm so sorry to refuse.

EDGAR. Well, I see you must, though I'm very sad you must.
But if later you should feel revived, or if
You found you could rest before dinner——

PERPETUA. It still has to be no, and still I'm sorry.

EDGAR. I can well imagine how tired you are. You can let
Your sleep make you a Hallowe'en instead.
Dreams know where to look for deeper and stranger
Shadows than I do. Horses, it always seems
To me, are half a dream, even when
You have them under your hand, and when I *dream* them
They tremble and sweat, the caves of their nostrils blowing
Bright clouds of breath, a foaming sea
Breaks against their mouths, their flanks are smoking
Like Abel's fire to heaven, as though
A dreadful necessity had ridden them hard
Through the miles of my sleep, all the benighted way
From legend into life. And then in the morning
There they are in the stables, waiting to be blessed.

PERPETUA. Show me these wonders.

EDGAR.   Now?

PERPETUA.   Yes, why not now?
All of us.

EDGAR.   That goes for you, papa.

DUKE. Invisibly I come.

EDGAR [*glumly*].   Invisibility
Makes you look younger than ever.

                              [*Exit* PERPETUA *and* EDGAR.

DUKE.   Jessie,
Will you make an end of dotting your *i*'s and join us?

JESSIE. Thank you, dear,
But I'd like to finish this letter to my father,
Even though he'll never read it.

DUKE.   Jessie, my love,
If he'll never read it, do you have to write so much?

JESSIE. Well, no, but he lives such a long way out of the village
I like to make it worth the postman's while.

Enter ROSABEL.

DUKE. Rosabel, where have you been mooning
All the long afternoon? Come with your friends
And look at horses. Edgar is showing Miss Reedbeck
Round the stables.

ROSABEL.   Yes, yes, I may follow you—
When do you mean to show her how to observe
The stars through your telescope? Is it to-night?

DUKE. No, not to-night; sometime, perhaps, or perhaps
Never; who can say?

ROSABEL.   .   But *you* will be there, I suppose.
Who is it that's mooning then? And all night long?
And making the world look small and apologetic
And as good as unpopulated? I hate your telescope!

DUKE. So you have said. Don't let it obsess you.
Look up, Mrs. Siddons, it's easy enough
To see over the top of a telescope. So try,
Or you'll soon make yourself ill. Anyway
I'm washing my hands of all the sky to-night,
And I'm going early to bed.

                                          [*Exit the* DUKE.

ROSABEL [*to herself*].   So no one at all
Will be there. Now I know why all day long

[56]

Life has been tilting and driving me towards
To-night. I'm not myself any more,
I am only the meaning of what comes after dark,
If I have the courage.

              [*She remembers* JESSIE *and turns to her.*

            Obsessed, obsessed.
It's very true. One thought in my head,
Persevering like someone running on a race-track;
When it seems to be going it's coming again.
I wrestle with it, and hold it close,
I can't let it go, nor laugh it away. Is this
How men get driven to send history lurching on
To God knows where? Nothing matters
Except that he should be made to feel. He hurts
Whoever he touches. He has to be touched by fire
To make a human of him, and only a woman
Who loves him can dare to do it.

JESSIE.   Listen, love,
You'll be sending yourself silly. I always think
When someone knocks you down, it doesn't improve things
To knock yourself up. The way a thing is, is often
The way you happen to look at it. He's as kind
As anybody living, if you take a running jump.
And if you only had a stamp we could go together
And put this in the box.

ROSABEL.   I'm over-run
By the most curious thoughts. I believe I was kept
From quite succeeding in anything I set
My heart on, so that now I should give all
My heart to this, to-night. The girl Perpetua
Has the courage that makes a person come true.
Did your hear her say how she went to war on things

She hated? I think she came to show me
What it is I have to do; indeed, I can't do less!
And nothing less will do to open his eyes
On to the distances that separate him
From other people.

JESSIE.   Look at me: I've put Cumberland
When I mean Northants.

ROSABEL.   To-night, no one is there.
You'll see, I shall send his Observatory
Where Nero's Rome has gone; I'll blaze a trail
That he can follow towards humanity!

JESSIE. Now I wonder who's the most likely person to have a
stamp?

THE CURTAIN FALLS

SCENE TWO

The Observatory Room at night. The DUKE *is lying on a day-bed in the
dark. Enter* PERPETUA. *The light from the corridor follows her
a little way into the room. She stands uncertain. The* DUKE
speaks from the darkness.

DUKE. And Endymion, when the moon had borne him
Fifty daughters, was rewarded with
An eternal siesta; his breast and belly rose
And fell like the sea; his breath played
All day with the motes of the dust,
While all about him suffered, withered, and crumbled
Into the dust his breath played with; only,
Between the slats of his perfect sleep
Came little slants of sun, and they were muddy
With the hard wading of humanity;

[58]

This made him change his position slightly,
And that stirred up the scent of the thyme which made
His unimpassioned bed.

PERPETUA.   It's rather frightening
When a dark room starts to speak.

DUKE.   My original
Syntax, like original sin, grows vastier
In the dark. Come in.

PERPETUA.   What does your legend mean?

DUKE. It means, Perpetua, we're all as well
As can be expected. Does anyone know you're here?

PERPETUA. No one.

DUKE.   They would think I meant to love you.
I wonder if I mean any such thing.
We'll make some light. Matches?

PERPETUA.   No.

DUKE. No, here are some.

[He lights an oil lamp.

                         This was the first
Astonishment of creation; after that
Came the frenzy of which you and I
Are the humble result. An access of starlight
And the fish began to swim; God gave way
To hallucinations; you and I again.
Would you like a drink?

PERPETUA.   Thank you. Tell me, as one
Hallucination to another, what
Happiness do you get up here with your telescope?

DUKE. I can't remember. That's a handsome moth
Come in to die, two petals, two tendrils,

[59]

And a flake of snow, meticulous, irrelevant,
Unwise. You came to see my stars. I have them
Here.

PERPETUA. I expect you can find your way about them
Even in the dark. Tell me who it is
We're trained on now.

DUKE.   Senator Saturn, white-
Hot with gravity. His moon, out of love
For his grey steel brow,
Streamed away her life into a circle
Of tormented arms. You see them there,
You see how they circle and never touch.
Saturn is alone, for all their circling round him.

PERPETUA. And alone so long. I'm looking at the same star
That shone alone in the wake of Noah's
Drifting ark as soon as the rain was over,
That shone on shining Charlemagne
Far away, and as clear
As the note of Roland's homing horn.
Alone so long, and now casually
Descending to us, on a Thursday midnight:
Saturn, who once glinted in the glass
Of Ariadne's mirror at the moment
When she died and melted out of Naxos.

DUKE. Ariadne died in childbirth. One
Life put the other out. It was Edgar's mode
Of entrance. Where in the sky shall we go to now?

PERPETUA. Wherever you may like to take me. I'm
A stranger here.

DUKE.   She died a girl in love,
And I went on in love without her

[60]

For longer than was fair. But this is not
Astronomy.

PERPETUA.   Astrology, then. You can't
Throw someone against the sky and not expect
A certain vapour of magic to condense
In moisture on their lashes. Let me believe
For a little while in man's ordeal by star
And tell me your own. I want to hear it.

DUKE. Isn't it a strange love, Perpetua,
That will never, can never, know what it was?
Death chose to interrupt us while we were still
Careening together high above the spires
Of common sense. And so what modulation
Would have come, how soon, how scaling down,
Is never to be known. And I can never tell
Whether a love, which was haled away
While it still was hale, was all and more
Of love than I could expect again: or if
The one twin-hearted permanence
Was waiting somewhere ahead. That has always
Perplexed me. What have I been doing, since
She died? Making do because the best
Was done? Or have I been turning head by head
To find the face which, willingly,
I should never let pass? For a long while now
I've been thinking the first, but to-day
The question seems to have sprung into life again.

PERPETUA. With your mind so full of inquiry, I'm surprised
You've had any time for love.

DUKE.   It takes no time.
It's on us while we walk, or in mid-sentence,

A sudden hoarseness, enough to choke the sense.
Now isn't that so?

PERPETUA.   Not so with me.

DUKE.   You must try
To use longer sentences. Then you would certainly feel
The fumbling in the quiver behind every syllable
And so to the arrow string, like a sudden
Swerving parenthesis.

PERPETUA.   Do you think I should?

DUKE. No doubt of it.

PERPETUA.   There isn't any reason
Why a sentence, I suppose, once it begins,
Once it has risen to the lips at all
And finds itself happily wandering
Through shady vowels and over consonants
Where ink's been spilt like rivers or like blood
Flowing for the cause of some half-truth
Or a dogma now outmoded, shouldn't go
Endlessly moving in grave periphrasis
And phrase in linking phrase, with commas falling
As airily as lime flowers, intermittently,
Uninterrupting, scarcely troubling
The mild and fragile progress of the sense
Which trills trebling like a pebbled stream
Or lowers towards an oath-intoning ocean
Or with a careless and forgetful music
Looping and threading, tuning and entwining,
Flings a babel of bells, a carolling
Of such various vowels the ear can almost feel
The soul of sound when it lay in chaos yearning
For the tongue to be created: such a hymn
If not as lovely, then as interminable,

As restless, and as heartless, as the hymn
Which in the tower of heaven the muted spheres
With every rippling harp and windy horn
Played for incidental harmony
Over the mouldering rafters of the world,
Rafters which seldom care to ring, preferring
The functional death-watch beetle, stark, staccato,
Economical as a knuckle bone,
Strict, correct, but undelighting
Like a cleric jigging in the saturnalia,
The saturnalia we all must keep,
Green-growing and rash with life,
Our milchy, mortal, auroral, jovial,
Harsh, unedifying world,
Where every circle of grass can show a dragon
And every pool's as populous as Penge,
Where birds, with taffeta flying, scarf the air
On autumn evenings, and a sentence once
Begun goes on and on, there being no reason
To draw to any conclusion so long as breath
Shall last, except that breath
Can't last much longer.

DUKE.   Now point me out the comma
Where you loved me.

PERPETUA.   Not at any.

DUKE.   Let me see;
Was there a colon somewhere?

PERPETUA.   Perhaps one;
But if so we passed it without any trouble
Of any sort.

DUKE.   Never mind. There are sure

[63]

To be other sentences. The little god
Is older than he was, and moves more slowly.

PERPETUA. Even when he aims at you?

DUKE.   For me, I'm afraid,
He makes a special effort, shoots
Most generously, and then, poor boy, can't handle
A bow for several weeks.

PERPETUA.   Why are you so sure
That I must love you? The field is wide,
And everyone's heart is a great eccentric;
Its whole distinction is a madness. Wildly
Away from any mark it goes, making
Anywhere the same gigantic mimicry of sunshine,
No one else knows why. Be sure of nothing.

DUKE. Do you know what night this is?

PERPETUA.   All-Hallows Eve.

DUKE. All-Hallows Eve. If the earth is ever wise
To magic, this is the night when magic's wisdom
Comes rolling in across our sedate equation.
All the closed hours unlock; the rigorous ground
Grows as soft as the sea, exhaling
The bloom of the dead everywhere. They almost
Live again: as nearly, at least, as we
Can brush on death. And through the night
They trespass agreeably on our time of trespasses,
Molesting the air in a pale, disinterested
Way, until they thankfully notice
The dark is paler, and sigh themselves out again;
Though not before they've planted, as they go,
A seed of chill which grows rapidly
Into a rigid winter where the sun

[64]

Can hardly raise himself to make a noon.
But still, that's presently. What's more to our purpose
Is that to-night the gravity of mirrors
Is so potent it can draw the future
Into the glass, and show shadows of husbands
To girls who sit and comb their hair. Suppose
You try it.

PERPETUA.   I'm two or three centuries
Too late.

DUKE.   We know nothing yet.
There's the mirror. In your bag no doubt
A comb. And while you comb tradition says
You must eat an apple: though God knows why
Any apple should trust itself between your teeth
After this morning's little episode.
However, here's one intrepid to the core.

PERPETUA. How old is this mirror? The glass
Is very loath to let me in.

DUKE.   Eight duchesses
Have rested there in passing, before the glass
Began to cloud; and after that came three
Peering housekeepers, a chambermaid
Who, what with frequent tears and the ageing mirror,
Never saw her face; and me, who by
Much early study have overcome the need
To try.

PERPETUA. And I am the eight duchesses
And the three housekeepers and the chambermaid
Combing their hair. I am any girl: Perpetua
Perpetual, making no gesture I can call
My own, engraving theirs one lifetime deeper.

[65]

Midnight, the apple, and Perpetua
Combing her hair, as all the time she was.

[*The* DUKE *quietly crosses the room until his reflection falls into the mirror.* PERPETUA'S *attention is caught; she stares into the glass before she turns suddenly to look at the* DUKE.

It seemed to be your son.

DUKE.   Perpetua,
You must play fair.

PERPETUA.   You must tell that to the mirror.
The reflection seemed to be Edgar.

DUKE.   Then the mirror
Is very penetrating. It has seen
How young, to all intents, I am.

PERPETUA.   I suppose so.
You think there's no magic.

DUKE.   That's as kind
As anything you've said. I think there *is*
Magic: an old dim-sighted mirror
And a shaded lamp for one genial moment
Raised me out of the falling leaves. A pity
The vision has gone. I'll agree to immortality
If immortality is to be always twenty-five
Seen by a man approaching fifty. The thought
Alone sends me begging to Olympus.
And you, being twenty-five, and looked upon
By me, together we make one golden flesh
For which both worlds, this and the next, will try
To outbid each other, and while the bidding mounts
We'll spend our love between them, disregarding
Both, until——

[66]

PERPETUA.   Until, next year,
  I am twenty-six.

DUKE.   Which is twenty-five and one more.
  I am the one.

PERPETUA.   It remains for me to love you.

DUKE. It has always been understood to be so easy.
  Why ever should you not? Am I, before
  God, too old? Consider the rocks
  Of Arizona, and then consider me.
  How recently the world has had the pleasure
  Of pleasing, the opportunity of knowing me.
  Age, after all, is only the accumulation
  Of extensive childhood: what we were,
  Never what we are. Don't deliver me
  Up to my grey hairs.

PERPETUA.   Them I could certainly
  Love. No, it's rather that I wonder
  Whether you're not almost too young to be lived with.

DUKE. When we're married I shall age beside you; forgive me
  Loitering now till you draw level.

PERPETUA. When we're married?

DUKE.   Are we to be formal?
  Should I have asked you first?

PERPETUA.   Not if you have
  Some other way of knowing the answer. Have you?

DUKE. Perhaps I may pass that question back. Have I?

PERPETUA. Your Grace——

DUKE.   Somewhere I have a Christian name.

PERPETUA. Do you know anything against my father?

DUKE. In my heart, nothing.
He loves me in his way, and that absolves him
From any defect on earth. No doubt
He'll have to stand in a corner of heaven with his face
To a jasper wall, but here let him thrive.

PERPETUA.   You mean
You know.

DUKE.   I know he wishes to make honey.
Any bee would tell you, that's impossible
If clover objects to rape.

PERPETUA.   So this is how
You know I shall marry you: for Poppadillo's sake?

DUKE. This is how.

PERPETUA.   And perhaps it is going to feel
Strange to you at first to know I am not.
No, no, you're mistaken, and I was quite
Mistaken, too! This isn't how I mean
To lose my way, by force of circumstantial
Evidence. When I lose my way I shall lose it
In my own time, and by my own misguided
Sense of direction.

DUKE.   Planting your own brambles,
Digging your own pitfalls, willing your own
Will-o'-the-wisps, designing
Down to the last detail Perpetua's Folly.

PERPETUA. Without respect of persons. But do you mean
You have sat perched up here, for months and years,
Your eyes shrewdly glittering with starlight,
Knowing that my father, fifty feet below,
Was being clever in your clover, and you said
Nothing?

[68]

DUKE.   We were being so happy together.
  And if I had mentioned it, he would have felt
  Obliged to discontinue, which would have been
  Immensely sad. And, what is more,
  Swarming stars and solitary Duke
  Would have been unvisited to-night.

PERPETUA. How happy do you feel to know you tried
  For a bride by this conspiracy of silence?

DUKE. How happy do you feel to know you were ready
  To take a husband to make that silence absolute?

PERPETUA. I made no pretence of loving you. I was glad
  When Edgar came to the mirror; I don't know why.

DUKE. I seem to have come to the end of myself
  Sooner than I expected. So there's to be
  No climax and adorable close
  With ego agonistes crowned and smiling?
  The strange charm of being alive breaks off
  Abruptly, with nothing determined, nothing solved,
  No absolute anything. I thought this time
  The ends of the ring would join. But, no,
  I'm back among the fragments.

PERPETUA.   Is this fair?

DUKE. How nature loves the incomplete. She knows
  If she drew a conclusion it would finish her.
  But, O God, for one round Amen!

PERPETUA.   That only
  Comes on judgement day, and so,
  As love won't live with judgement, Amen must wait.
  Show me one more star and I must go.

DUKE. I think they're falling.

While I love you without being loved they're sure
To be restive.

PERPETUA.   When they fall do they scorch the air
In passing? Is that what I can smell?

DUKE.   Or is it
The smell of man being born to trouble? Or both
The upward sparks and the downward stars together?

PERPETUA. Something *is* on fire. I can hear the flames
Crunching on wood.

DUKE.   Have my almost mindless gardeners
Been suddenly visited by imagination
And lit us a Hallowe'en bonfire?

PERPETUA.   Why, look, the garden's
Capering with light. The fire is underneath us—
Look! It's the house, this wing of the house is on fire!

DUKE. Merciful heaven,
Wouldn't you think my blood was warm enough
To get us through a night without encouragement?

PERPETUA. Shall we be able to get away?

DUKE.   By all means.
We'll leave the moths to perform whatever
Immolation is necessary. A more
Temperate life is better for us,
And the cooler coast of the garden.

          [*He throws open the door and looks on to the stairs.*

Well, here's a riproaring gauntlet to be run
By a couple of God's children.

PERPETUA.   No! No, no!
Not that way!

DUKE.   Which other? The only alternative
To downward is upward, and how do you propose
Two such wingless babes as we are—
No, Perpetua; quickly, love, before
The even chance is out of patience with us.

PERPETUA. No! There's no chance there. You can see
There's no chance there. It's all in the fire,
Every tread of the stairs. What shall we do?

               [*She runs to the window and looks down.*

So far away, so far away.

DUKE.   Trust me;
Try this way in my arms, Perpetua. Hope
Is forlorn, but I'm sure very fond of us.
We'll give her the benefit, shall we, and both be brave?

PERPETUA. Don't make me. I'd rather jump to the garden, and die
Fair and broken. I'll make my own death
As it suits me.

DUKE.   That as well? I'm sorry; you can have
Your own way in everything else.

PERPETUA.   Please,
Please, please, please.

DUKE.   Well, I see
We've chosen. Hope has got tired of waiting
And taken half the staircase with her. Now,
We'll ring a rescue, and then indulge in the luxury
Of having nothing to do but fold our hands.

         [*He holds her beside him while he uses the telephone.*

Gently, my dear, you White Queen; nothing
Has hurt us yet. A fire at Stellmere Park.
Two people trapped: neither anxious to die.

[71]

I suggest you should make remarkable speed.
God bless you. They didn't wait for blessing.

PERPETUA. Aren't you desperate, too? Aren't you even afraid?

DUKE. Why, yes, yes, I have to be; I love myself,
And I shall be sad to say good-bye to myself;
There's no one like me, though so many better.
Will you kiss the last of a singular man?

PERPETUA. Easily, oh, easily.

DUKE.   There's always a good thing left
Even when the world would seem to be spent out.
Do you think you love me?

PERPETUA.   Yes, I love you:
Between the giddiness I love you.

DUKE.   May it also
Be between my arms? I love my love
With a death because it has no alteration
And no end. This concluding grace, Amen.
In the long world we're being shaken from
The star which, when it's rising, is called Venus,
Setting is Lucifer, the goddess
Graduating into demon, and what good
Is that for a man's immortal spirit? But you
And I, pursuing love no farther than this
Pure outcry of recognition,
Possess it most faithfully.

PERPETUA.   I only know—
Listen to the fire now, listen to it!
It means to let nothing escape. I only know
We go together into pain.

DUKE. Out of the world like snow. And so
The phoenix and the turtle did.

[72]

Pain took them, too, and welded them
And melted them, and made a union
Of beauty born and beauty reft away,
And, when the air was empty, time was brimming,
And light was beating with one heart.

PERPETUA. I'm afraid of the fire, I'm afraid, I am so
Afraid of the fire.

[*The voice of* REDDLEMAN *is heard outside the door.*

REDDLEMAN [*off*]. Your Grace! All right, all right, your Grace!

DUKE. The voice of to-morrow morning, after all.
We're not to be allowed perfection, Perpetua.
The kind world intervenes.

Enter REDDLEMAN.

REDDLEMAN. Ah, you poor sinners. I'm with you now;
Did you think I was never coming?

PERPETUA.   Never coming,
Never, never coming!

DUKE.   Quietly yet,
Fly up gently, we've still got far to go.
How do you propose to rescue us, Reddleman?
And how the hell did you got here?

REDDLEMAN: By me flair
For elementary science. I thumbed a lift
On the rising heat. And, by the blistering
Of the blessed St. Laurence and the blessed St. Vincent,
Shadrac, Meshac, Abednego, and all
The sainted salamanders, I've got me nerve again;
For there's the conflagration below, frumping
And grouching like all the golden lads of lions
I ever put me hand into the fire of!

[73]

Didn't God make sinners of you and trap you her
For the decent purpose of putting me back
In the way of salvation?

DUKE.   And us, too, I hope.
Can we go the way you came?

PERPETUA.   God be kind,
Be kind.

REDDLEMAN. Have you any objection, now,
To dropping from time to time into me arms
From a great way off? 'Twould be to avoid the stairs,
Themselves being gone entirely.

PERPETUA. Must it be that way?

REDDLEMAN.   In the Captain's keeping,
Via Leo, con brio, the way of the lions!

DUKE. He's got himself well up in the god class now,
Perpetua: all we have to do is trust ourselves
To the rope of his nerve, spit on our hands, and go.

[BATES *appears at the window.*

BATES. Well, *you've* got yourselves in a picklin' walls-up
And no mistake.

DUKE.   Are we to have all
The guardian angels at a blow?
You spoil us, Bates.

REDDLEMAN.   He spoils me night of glory.
Send him about his business, if you love me,
Your Grace, for the love of God, send him
About his business!

BATES.   Couldn't the Lord Lieutenant
Even keep his nose out of this little job?

[74]

Come on, miss; come and take a butcher's
At the panorama; it's lovely outside 'ere.

PERPETUA. Oh, yes, yes!

REDDLEMAN.   Monkeys, monkeys, monkeys!

DUKE. How do you think we're going to get down, Bates?

BATES. Well, I come up by the ladders, but according
To the rules we have to slip down by the snakes. Still,
Do what your fancy tells you, mate. I'm
Not looking.

PERPETUA.   And I wish I hadn't looked, and I wish
We were safe on the ground.

DUKE.   Think of something high
Like Kanchenjunga. That very nearly takes us
Down the ladder before we start.

REDDLEMAN.   Your Grace,
You're not so out of your mind as to go
Out of the window? Encouraging robbery
And violence, you are, to set your foot
On a ladder propped up against your property
Without permission, and in the middle of the night
When no decent man would be lashing one ladder
To another, and he in his shirt.

BATES.   You save 'em
Wiv your trousers, go on, let's see you; save 'em wiv your
trousers.

DUKE. Reddleman, by all means love your lions,
But condescend to the snakes. Come on.

REDDLEMAN. Where's a fine soul under heaven?

DUKE.   Not playing
With fire, wherever else he may be.

[75]

BATES.   That's right, miss,
Let me take you, miss; fink nuffing of it.
Relax yourself, as though you was mink.
Fink lovely foughts, miss, and you won't weigh nuffing.
Wonder what stretch I'll have to do for abduction?

DUKE [*climbing through the window after them*]. A beautiful room,
Reddleman; worth a fortune
In memories and astronomical equipment.

[*He disappears from view.* REDDLEMAN *leans out.*

REDDLEMAN. H'wot do you think the dear God gave me back
Me nerve for? To come crawling after heathen
Like spittle down a window? B'Jason,
I've a better opinion of meself.
Anyway, it makes me giddy and it's no position
For any reasonable man to get himself into.

[*He crosses the room, throws open the door, and meets the
glare of the fire.*

Tossing your mighty manes, roaring yellow murder!
The Captain's not afraid!

[*Exit* REDDLEMAN. *The* DUKE *climbs back in at the window calling him, races across the room to the door, calls:*

DUKE. Reddleman, you hell-raking maniac!

[*He picks up the half-eaten apple from the dressing table, calls
to* REDDLEMAN:

Who would have the heart to disappoint you?

[*He puts the apple between his teeth and follows* REDDLE-
MAN *the way of the stairs.*

THE CURTAIN FALLS ON ACT TWO

[76]

ACT THREE

*The Temple of the Ancient Virtues, an hour or so later. The light from
the burning house reflected in the lake.* ROSABEL *is sobbing in the
dark. Enter* DOMINIC, *carrying two chairs and a stable lantern.
He halts and listens to the sobbing.*

DOMINIC. May I interrupt your unhappiness,
Just to bring in one or two things? It's begun
To rain. Everything's going to get wet.
I wonder if you need cry quite so despairingly.
It makes me feel very awkward. I am not good
At comforting people, even when I know
Where to look for them. I'm Dominic Reedbeck . . .
How do you do? And where would you be?

ROSABEL.   Oh, no,
Don't look for me.

DOMINIC.   I couldn't look for you;
I don't know who you are. Everyone
Is safe, you know; they're all accounted for,
Except Miss Fleming. Do you know where she is?

ROSABEL. No. No one must ever see her again.

DOMINIC. Why not? Is she so badly burned? What is it,
Oh, what *is* it? I wish you'd help me to be helpful;
I find it so difficult.

ROSABEL.   I'm here. I wish
I were dead.

DOMINIC.   I don't see how you can wish for something
You only know the name of. Now that it's raining

[77]

I won't be the only one coming in here. Perhaps
You should try to feel better. If I were you.

ROSABEL. They wouldn't look for me in hell.

DOMINIC.   Oh, yes, they would.
It's the obvious place to look for anyone,
If you're speaking euphemistically.

ROSABEL. I'm grateful to you. So would anyone
In hell be. Your voice is very cold.
I want harshness. I want hatred.
If you would hate me it might help me to bear
To think of myself. You're going to find it easy.
It was I who started the fire. I did it
Deliberately.

DOMINIC.   Perpetua was there.
The Duke was there. They might never have got away.

ROSABEL. But you haven't understood. You can't have understood.
It was I who did this unimaginable thing.

DOMINIC. I was thinking of myself.
My sister was there because I sent her there.
Perhaps you were compelled to be the means
By which I was shown I had fallen into error.
If so, I must thank you. Thank you, Miss Fleming.

ROSABEL. You're mad! Do you think I hurled myself away
From all the decent world for your sake?
Hate me, hate me! Oh, why is it
You won't understand?

DOMINIC.   I do understand. I know
Too well our preternatural aptitude
For sin. My father made it quite clear to me.

ROSABEL. Oh, what shall I do?

[78]

DOMINIC.   There's Sergeant Harry Bullen,
The policeman from Swinford Magna. He's a very
Reasonable chap; I'm sure he'd arrest you
Willingly if you went and asked him.
And he's here, which is very convenient for you.

ROSABEL. Yes, where? Where is he?

DOMINIC.   I saw him five minutes ago,
Coming head first down a ladder, to show the Duke
(As he said) that in the ordinary course of living
It makes little difference which way up you are.
He was joking, I think.

ROSABEL.   I'll find him, and give myself up.
Yes, up, out of this ditch of despair. No one
Need think of me again. I hardly remember
What I was like before to-day, but I think
I was an ordinary woman. No one
Else will remember. 'She was always demented!'
It isn't true: never; until to-day
Struck me like a tornado, God knows from where.
But now I shall give myself up. Do I look
Plain and frightful? It could scarcely matter
Less. But, please God, help me avoid the Duke,
Wherever he may be.

Enter the DUKE, *carrying things salvaged from the fire and over his
shoulders a string of Chinese lanterns.*

DUKE.   He's down at the Temple,
I think, putting up some lanterns which he found
In a box. You'll find him there, presumably
Intent on some small ceremony of his own,
Though fairly uncertain whether it's obsequies
Or jubilation; he's in two hearts about it,

[79]

And both weigh heavier than the one he had.
God bless you, Rosabel; hold these; for a time
We thought we had lost you.

ROSABEL.   Did you think so? Lost me?

DOMINIC. You must tell him now. It will be much easier now;
No postponing.   [*Exit* DOMINIC.

DUKE.   It's important that we should offset the smacking of the
     furies
With a little decorous gaiety, with a show
Of holier, if also homelier, flames.
The lanterns, Rosabel. They'll be very pale
Compared with the foment of wild flamboyant rose
We have in the sky to-night; but never mind;
Think what deeds of spring are done
By the glow-worm light of a primrose.

ROSABEL. I started the fire.

DUKE.   How did you come to do that?
A careless flash from your incendiary eyes,
Perhaps.

ROSABEL. You must believe me. I fired the wing,
To destroy the observatory, to make you human,
To bring you down to be among the rest of us,
To make you understand the savage sorrows
That go on below you. To-day, this awful day,
The violence of a long unhappiness rocked
And fell, and buried me under itself at last.
How vile it was I know. I know for life.
But I didn't know you were there; believe me, I didn't
Know any living soul was there!

DUKE.   O,
O, O, O, Rosabel:

[80]

If you had only asked me first.
I could have told you no fire would be enough
To burn down heaven, and while it's there
I shall find some wide-eyed place where I can sit
And scrutinize the inscrutable, amazed
That we can live in such a condition of mystery
And not be exasperated out of our flesh,
As we might be, were it not that flesh
Is interesting, too.
Your fire was too small, Rosabel, though enough
To singe my butler into ecstasy,
And smoke tears into eyes unaccustomed to them,
Mine, I mean. So much I delighted in
Is now all of ash, like a dove's breast feathers
Drifting dismally about the garden.

ROSABEL. Time and I both know how to bring
Good things to a bad end, all
In the course of love. No wonder
'God be with you' has become 'Good-bye',
And every day that wishes our welfare says
Farewell. To-night will go past, as a swan
Will pass like a recurring dream
On the light sleep of the lake,
And I shall be smoothed away in the wake of the swan;
But I can never return what I've lost you, or lose
What I gave, though the long steadiness of time
May long to make us well.

DUKE. So much I delighted in is all of ash.

> [ROSABEL, *giving a moan almost too low to hear, goes out.*
> *Her place is taken by* PERPETUA, *but the* DUKE, *now hanging*
> *the lanterns, hasn't seen the change.*

[81]

But the lost world of walls and stairs,
Where I could cosset ghosts for their melancholy
Charm, has let the daylight into me
With a straight left of love. So no remorse,
Rosabel. I love my love, and my love loves me.
Everything goes but everything comes.
We fall away into a future, and all
The seven seas, and the milky way
And morning, and evening, and hi-cockalorum are in it.
Nothing is with the past except the past.
So you can make merry with the world, Rosabel.
My grateful thanks.

PERPETUA. I have to make you understand.

DUKE.   I forgive you:
You can mine the lake so that it bursts
In a hundred and one torrential rainbows
Over the roof of the Carpenters' Arms; you can shatter
Conservatories into a deluge of crystal,
And shoot the cowman's nine insufferable
Children: I forgive you in advance.
I've achieved the rare, benevolent place
Where the irk of the lonely human state
Is quite unknown, and the fumbling fury
We call our life—It wasn't Rosabel
Who spoke then. It was surely Perpetua?

PERPETUA. I have to make you understand. You must
Be patient with me.

DUKE.   God so, it's the little firebird.
Are you rested? Lanterns, you see, to light our love.
I thought we could sit by the cinders
And toast our hearts, if Bates, as he was told to,
Brings the champagne.

[82]

PERPETUA.   You have to give me
　Your best and gentlest attention. Be
　At your most understanding. I need it, if I don't
　Deserve it from you. To-night, when we seemed
　Closely, and only us of all the living
　World, attended by a dragon breathing out
　Almost certain death——

Enter BATES, *with champagne and glasses in a basket, and carrying*
another lantern.

BATES.   That Captain Reddleman,
　As he likes to demean hisself to call hisself—
　Now you're not getting yourselves into anuvver
　Critical situation? You can scramble down
　Off of that one on your own
　Virgin initiative; I'm badgered if I'm going
　To throw anuvver expensive rescue party.

DUKE. Matches, Perpetua?

PERPETUA.   No.

BATES.   His illuminated
　Lordship Reddleman should ought to have
　His brain looked into. In and out, in and out,
　In and out of the burning building, like
　A perishing nigger in and out of a flaming
　Woodpile. And what he says about me's
　Enough to arrest a cock in the middle of his crow
　And bring a blush to his ruddy comb. It isn't
　The language I've been brought up to.

DUKE [*lighting the lanterns*].   The first astonishment
　Of creation; after that came the frenzy.

PERPETUA.   Let me
　Talk to you.

[83]

BATES.   Here's his incandescent majesty
Coming now, wiv his head under the table.

Enter REDDLEMAN, *carrying a table on his head*.

What's the matter, mate; lost your tit-fer?

REDDLEMAN. There's no doubt at all Your Grace has noticed
There are some men are born too small in the soul
To do gratifying deeds, and not sprain all decency.
And 'tis the footman Bates
Who's the diminuendo of all small souls.
He's a demi-semi soul, and that's magnanimous.
I have to put on me glasses, and then search
As though I was after looking for a louse
In Molly O'Magan's obster-eperous hair.
Would it be here you were wanting the table set up,
Your Grace?

DUKE.   Put it where the wind won't blow;
It's blowing cold. And for Christmas' sake
Will you pair of immortals kiss each other
And come off the tiles?

BATES. I'd just like to know who give him permission
To go measuring my soul? I never done.
I've got it nicely laid away: spotless,
Wiv lavender.

REDDLEMAN.   'Twas a mighty night of miracle,
With Cuchulain at me right hand, and Daniel at me left,
And the smallest soul in the world dashes it from me,
And he naked in his shirt.

DUKE.   Ah, miracles, Reddleman,
Miracles; don't trust them. How far
Can a man journey on a miracle? It's better

[84]

To bounce your behind on any spavined hack
Than to straddle a flash of lightning.
Straighten your laurel wreaths, the couple of you,
And remember one another in your prayers.
It seems I have something else to listen to.

Enter REEDBECK *and* DOMINIC.

REEDBECK. Ah, here he is. I'm not what you thought me, your
    Grace.
    I must tell you plainly I'm not at all what you thought me.

DUKE. No?

REEDBECK. No. If you ask these men to go, your Grace,
    I shall be only too grieved to tell you what I am.

BATES [*to* REEDDLEMAN]. Nuffing to stay for, boy. I'll come and
    see you
    Popping yourself in and out of the fire again.

REDDLEMAN. Breakfast, your Grace, at what o'clock?

DUKE.   The morning
    Must wait, Reddleman. I have still
    The rest of the night to consider.

                       [*Exeunt* BATES *and* REDDLEMAN.

PERPETUA [*to* REEDBECK].   Darling,
    Not now. Any day or night of the year,
    There's always time, you can go together, and look
    At the pigs or the winter wheat, and talk your two
    Hearts out; but just this night, and for just
    These five minutes of this night, leave me
    To talk to him alone.

REEDBECK.   I've worked myself up,
    I've reached the pitch now; it would never do
    To put it—put it off; walked much too fast,
    Breath very short, and then heart very heavy,

Imagination—disconcerting—too vivid: I see you
Both up there, no amount of stars
Any use, in dreadful danger, and who but me,
I, whichever it is, responsible?

DOMINIC. Please blame me for that. Do allow me
To know which sin belongs to whom. We shall only
Get confused, father, unless you keep strictly
To your own wrong turning.

REEDBECK.   Extremely difficult
To know where to stop, once you begin to believe
You're not all you should be. Let me see,
There was something worse Dominic said
I had to confess to you.

PERPETUA.   He knows, he knows.
So now, you poor worried Poppadillo, half
Awash with sleep, you can go back
To bed at once, or else I think I shall cry.

REEDBECK. But I don't quite know what you know he knows,
And I think I'd better——

DUKE.   Drink, Reedbeck, I think
You'd better drink. We have something to celebrate,
You and I, which lights me more than the most
Tower-toppling blaze that ever lit
A city lane——

PERPETUA.   Oh, do let me speak to you!

REEDBECK. I've reached the pitch. I've worked myself up
To the point of whatever the point was when I first
Came in. But you're quite right, half awash, suddenly
Woken up in alarm——

DOMINIC.   Now, *think* a minute.

[86]

DUKE. Master Dominic: pass to your saintly father
     This glass of champagne.

REEDBECK.   Excuse me. But I know
     There's some good reason why I shall have to refuse.
     Now that my attention has been drawn
     To what must be a myopia in my moral vision—
     Must have been suffering from it all my life,
     I suppose: and to-night feels very latter-day;
     Wrath of God: here we are
     Looking such weak vessels and so temporary
     Among the four terrible elements
     (The rain and the firemen's hose remind me of the fourth)—
     What was I going to say? Yes, yes, I think
     It wouldn't be correct to drink with you before
     I give myself up to Sergeant Bullen.

DUKE.   Drink up,
     And keep your sins for some leisurely angel;
     They've nothing to do with me. Dominic,
     If what appear to be discrepancies
     In your father's books afflict you, let me tell you
     Though they seem unusual they're as much in order
     As Sergeant Bullen's collar and tie. There exists
     A document assigning to your father
     All those percentages from rents and sales
     Which you seem to have thought are misbegotten.

DOMINIC. Do you mean you've noticed the discrepancies
     And legalized them?

DUKE.   My dear conscience-nudging,
     Parent-pesting, guilt-corroded child,
     If I may address you with so much affection,
     The arrangement was perfect. It embarrassed
     Neither of us. Take a drink to wash

Your conscience down. And one brimming for you,
A pale representation of my heart,
Perpetua.

PERPETUA.   It's too full, seriously,
Far too full. You've been good to my father.
Please will you put it down? I know my hand
Isn't steady enough to take it.

DUKE.   Then let me sip
Some away from the western rim
And leave the east for you.

REEDBECK.   Made it legal?

DUKE. There now. Shall we drink
To the babe born in the fire, the crowning of souls
In extremity? As long as we live, Perpetua,
We shall be able to tell how, at midnight,
We skated over death's high-lit ebony
And heard the dark ring a change of light,
While everywhere else the clocks
Were sounding the depths of a dark, unhappy end.
And then we shall be able to say
How an autumn duke——

PERPETUA.   —found that fear could seem
Like love to a silly girl, who now knows
It was fear and not love, wishes you to forgive her,
Wishes she could sink away with the night
Where she won't any more trouble you.

DUKE [*after a long pause, raising his glass*]. Then the toast is: Fear.

PERPETUA. I had to tell you.

DUKE.   Do I
Have to drink alone?

[88]

PERPETUA.   No. No.

[They all drink in silence.

DUKE. Do you think I can't forgive you? I forgive
  Both of us for being born of the flesh,
  Which means I forgive all tossing and turning,
  All foundering, all not finding,
  All irreconcilability,
  All the friction of this great orphanage
  Where no one knows his origin and no one
  Comes to claim him. I forgive even
  The unrevealing revelation of love
  That lifts a lid purely
  To close it, and leaves us knowing that greater things
  Are close, but not to be disclosed
  Though we die for them. I forgive
  Everything, my most dear Perpetua,
  Except that I wasn't born something less ambitious,
  Such as a Muscovy duck.

REEDBECK.   I couldn't think
  Of allowing such generosity. Legalized!
  No, your Grace, I simply couldn't accept it.

DUKE. Reedbeck, my God! For how many years have you
  Stood here? You must be very old by now.
  I remember you well in happier times.

PERPETUA.   Poppadillo,
  Why do we all have to get between someone else
  And the sun? Keep me from doing this again.

REEDBECK. Whatever you say, my dear; though whatever you're
    saying
  I really don't know. I'd like to help, but you're both
  Talking in my sleep, evidently.

[89]

Enter EDGAR, JESSIE, *and* HILDA.

EDGAR. That was a hideous mile or two of driving!
  We saw the fire on the clouds, and guessed
  It could only be here.

HILDA.   I saw it from home, reflected
  In my bedroom window. I tried to telephone
  But I couldn't get through.

DUKE.   I must ask you, if you will,
  To remember we've been appreciating this very
  Minor act of God for more than two hours.
  The earth has moved on roughly a hundred
  And thirty thousand miles since then,
  And histories have been much altered.
  I hope the dance was a great success.

JESSIE.   Yes, lovely,
  But it's doing myself a great kindness to be able
  To sit down. Dancing all hours, and a couple of miles
  Of apprehension makes All Hallowe'en
  Into a marathon if a girl's not quite
  As hale and hallow as once she was.
  Is everybody safe?

DUKE.   Safe: I'll not say
  'As houses', considering what goes on,
  But as safe and suffering as health can be.

HILDA. It's a fortunate thing that providence
  Was in her friendly mood to-night
  And kept you out of Galileo's lap.

DUKE. Not she. She saw two souls there, happily occupied
  At the narrow end of the telescope,
  Two star-loving minutiae, male and female,
  Perpetua and my unoffending self:

[90]

And instantly shot out a vituperative
Tongue. And we were rescued by two
Heavenly agents, Bates and Reddleman.

REEDBECK. God bless them; I've never liked either of them,
But God bless them.

HILDA. And keep them in the heavenly business.

JESSIE. I'll kiss them for it presently. They must
Have got a bit above themselves
To rescue you from there.

EDGAR. And so
You meant to meet there, even this afternoon.
And the only comfort I had, all the way home,
Was that Perpetua was safely sleeping
Away in another house.

PERPETUA. We meant to meet there,
And this afternoon we were lying to you,
And never was a lie less happy for everyone.

DUKE. I hear me whistling down the wind.

JESSIE. We wouldn't
Like you to think we're setting up in competition,
But in our own small way we've met
With a catastrophe, too.

HILDA. Both our cars
Swung in at the gates together, and as our attention
Was all on the fire——

JESSIE. Our wings aren't what they were,
As Lucifer said after his long day's fall.

DUKE. What's the matter with the Fates to-day; fidget, fidget;
Why can't they settle down to some useful spinning?
I forgot to ask you, Hilda (Jessie and Lucifer
Remind me), how is Roderic?

HILDA.   Asleep when I left.
    Two ribs broken, and a slight concussion,
    Nothing worse. But that was enough to show me
    How bad it is to see Roderic hurt, but how
    Intolerable it would be to see Roderic
    Maimed, or dying day by day; and I sat
    Beside him and marvelled, and wondered how
    So much could lie there in a human shell,
    The long succession of life that led to him,
    Uninterrupted from the time
    Of time's aching infancy;
    In the beginning was Roderic; and now
    Haunting the same shell, were a childhood
    And a manhood, half a hundred years
    Of sights and sounds which once echoed and shone
    And now may only exist in him. And though
    He tries to be a copy of all his kind
    How can he be? He is Roderic-phenomenon,
    Roderic only, and at present Roderic in pain.
    I felt I must tell you so. This afternoon
    I made a cockshy of him, but this afternoon
    I could no more truly see him than he, poor darling,
    Can truly see half that there is to see.
    I must get back home. I only wanted to be
    Quite certain no one was hurt.

DUKE.   Rosabel
    Is hurt.

EDGAR.   But we saw her with Harry Bullen;
    She seemed most vigorous, talking his helmet off;
    He was mopping his head with a handkerchief.

DUKE.   Rosabel,
    Why? With Harry Bullen? Why should she be?

[92]

DOMINIC. Because she thought it was necessary
  To her peace of mind. She has given herself up.

DUKE. And I give you up! How, by hell's grand canyon,
  Do you know she has?

DOMINIC.   She was really very unhappy;
  I think I helped her to decide.

JESSIE.   But why?
  Given herself up for lost, or what?

DUKE.   You strapping,
  Ice-cold, donkey-witted douche of tasteless water!
  I could willingly—Dominic, dear boy,
  God would tell me He loves you, but then God
  Is wonderfully accomplished, and to me
  You seem less lovely, and for this good reason:
  You think more of the sin than of the sinner.
  Poor Rosabel. Where shall we find her?

HILDA.   When
  We saw them they were standing by the sundial.
  What has she done?

DUKE.   Loved me beyond her strength.
  We go and get her out of the arms of the law,
  However attractive Bullen's arms may be.
  Dear Rosabel! And after that we must find
  Beds for ourselves away from the smell of smouldering
  Memory. Bring along some of the lanterns.
  Excellent, blessed Rosabel. Ros-a-bel!

          [*He goes, calling her.* HILDA *follows him.*

REEDBECK [*to* JESSIE]. Beds, yes, yes, beds, quite important.
  There's one at least at my house if you'd care to oblige it,
  Care to make use of it. No more sleep for me
  To-night; it wouldn't be wise; I've only just

[93]

Managed to digest the sleep I've had already.
In something of a fuddle.

JESSIE.   Dear, I'd get
Into anybody's bed to-night, and sleep
Without a murmur, even in the arms of Morpheus
If he'd give up his lute and let me. Where's the step?

> [*She goes out,* REEDBECK *holding a lantern for her, and he
> follows her.*

DOMINIC. A fine rain raining still. Aren't you coming,
Perpetua?

PERPETUA.   I'll stay in the dry and rest.

DOMINIC. I was hoping to talk to you, to tell you, to say
How responsible I feel for all that fear
And danger, I mean yours to-night. I expect
You think I was very much to blame.

PERPETUA.   No,
Dominic.

DOMINIC. They think I'm altogether wrong,
All the time. But I don't know how that can be.
And yet the whole of life is so unconsidering,
Bird, beast, and fish, and everything,
I wonder how the Creator came to be
Mixed up in such company. Do you think I'm wrong?

PERPETUA. No, Dominic.

DOMINIC [*with a sigh*].   Ethics are very difficult.

> [*He goes into the rain, leaving* PERPETUA *and* EDGAR.
> *They sit in silence for a moment.*

EDGAR. Did you forget I was here?

[94]

PERPETUA. I didn't forget.
But I wish I could forget, and I wish you had forgotten,
This afternoon's brazen lying.

EDGAR. I have forgotten.
Why should we remember this afternoon
When probably no one else does?

PERPETUA. But am I sure
I want you to forget as incuriously as that?
I want your father not to be hurt by to-night,
I want you not to be hurt by this afternoon,
I want to be free to make my own way,
But I want to be remembered.

EDGAR. My memory
Is for nothing else. But, as it happens,
I hardly need it. Over and over again
I see you for the first time. I round
Some corner of my senses, and there, as though
The air had formed you out of a sudden thought,
I discover you. Any memory I had
Vanishes, to let you in so unannounced
My whole body stammers with surprise.
I imagine I love you. And I don't think
You can fairly object, when all you have to do
Is walk freely through my thoughts and round
My heart. You needn't even turn your head.

PERPETUA. Don't say this now. I'm still remembering
I can give pain, and that in itself is loss
Of liberty.

EDGAR. No, I just mentioned it in passing.

PERPETUA. No one is separate from another; how difficult
That is. I move, and the movement goes from life

[95]

To life all round me. And yet I have to be
Myself. And what is *my* freedom becomes
Another person's compulsion. What are we to make
Of this dilemma?

EDGAR.   I haven't the sense to ask.
Whatever the human mystery may be
I am it.

PERPETUA. There's comfort in that.

EDGAR.   Tell me:
Do I seem to you to be only a sort
Of postscript to my father?

PERPETUA.   No, Edgar,
Across and across my heart, never at all.

EDGAR. I begin to notice myself, too,
I must say. Here the little parents come.

Enter the DUKE *and* REEDBECK.

So now the house goes with a dragging wing.
Are your spirits very heavy, father?

DUKE.   They ride;
No, no, they ride well enough.

REEDBECK [*to* PERPETUA].   Isn't it time
My all night wanderer went to bed?

DUKE.   She will stay
For a moment's peaceful conversation.

PERPETUA. I want to know about Rosabel. When Dominic
said——

DUKE. I'll keep her story for a rainy day.

[96]

EDGAR. And for now the rain has blown over. Shall we go
     And see how the last of the flames dance down
     To sleep among the ruins, Perpetua?

DUKE. Our peaceful conversation, Perpetua.

EDGAR. Perpetua?

PERPETUA.   I'll find my way to bed.

EDGAR. I shall take the liberty to light you there.
     To-morrow, then, father.

DUKE.   To-morrow to you.

PERPETUA. To-morrow to us all, but not too soon.
     I need the soft pillows to make my peace
     Before I trust myself to another day to-morrow.

     [*Exeunt* EDGAR *and* PERPETUA. REEDBECK *is almost asleep
     in a chair.*

DUKE. Shall I be sorry for myself? In mortality's name
     I'll be sorry for myself. Branches and boughs,
     Brown hills, the valleys faint with brume,
     A burnish on the lake; mile by mile
     It's all a unison of ageing,
     The landscape's all in tune, in a falling cadence,
     All decaying. And nowhere does it have to hear
     The quips of spring, or, when so nearing its end,
     Have to bear the merry mirth of May.
     How fortunate to grow in the crow-footed woods,
     Eh, Reedbeck? But I see you're anxious to sleep.

REEDBECK. I? No, no; I'll never go to sleep
     Again to-night, much too disturbed.
     Don't know what to suggest I make of anything.
     I only hope a quiet dignity
     Will meet the case. Civilization is simply
     (If I had to define it) simply dignity,

Simply simple dignity; but then
Sons and daughters come into it, most lovable,
Most difficult, and unexpected combustion,
And so forth and so forth. Now le Roi Soleil,
How many children did he have? One legitimate,
Several illegitimate . . . le Duc de Maine,
La Duchesse de Chartres. . . .

DUKE.   Shall I be happy for myself?
In the name of existence I'll be happy for myself.
Why, Reedbeck, how marvellous it is to moulder.
Think how you would have felt when you were lying
Grubbing in your mother's womb,
With only a wall to look at,
If you could have seen in your embryonic eye
The realm of bryony, sloes, rose-hips,
And a hedge's ruin, a golden desuetude,
A countryside like a drowned angel
Lying in shallow water, every thorn
Tendering a tear. Think, Reedbeck,
Think of the wonder of such glimmering woe;
How in a field of milk-white haze the lost
Apollo glows and wanders towards noon;
The wind-blown webs are brighter,
The rolling apples warmer than the sun.
Heavens! you would have cried, the womb
Echoing round you: These are the heavens, and I,
Reedbeck, am stillborn. Would you not?

REEDBECK [*waking slightly*]. And la Duchesse de Condé, I think.

DUKE. So with ourselves; imagine: to have the sensation
Of nearness of sight, shortness of breath,
Palpitation, creaking in the joints,
Shootings, stabbings, lynching of the limbs,

[98]

A sudden illumination of lumbago.
What a rich world of sensation to achieve,
What infinite variety of being.
Is it not?

REEDBECK. Dominic not fond . . .
Perpetua. . . .

DUKE.   Reedbeck, I have to tell you
I mean to marry. I can still remember,
In my ebbing way, how pleasant it is to love;
An ancient love can blow again, like summer
Visiting St. Martin. A breath will do it,
If the breath comes deep, and deep it has come.
You must give me your felicitations. I marry
Rosabel, when Rosabel
(After six months, I understand)
Is disengaged from custody.

                    [*Only deep breathing comes from* REEDBECK.

Thank you, dear fellow. Rosabel
Would thank you, too, if she were here.
She and I, sharing two solitudes,
Will bear our spirits up to where not even
The nightingale can know,
Where the song is quiet, and quiet
Is the song. Tell me, Reedbeck, before
We leave each other in sleep, where would you say
The lonely moment is coaxing us to go?

                    [REEDBECK *gives a gentle near-whistling snore.*

Well, yes, yes, quite so, my little one,
It comes to that in the end.

THE CURTAIN FALLS FINALLY